When You and I Were Young, Whitefish

Dorothy M. Johnson

MOUNTAIN PRESS PUBLISHING COMPANY
Missoula, Montana

Portions of this book previously appeared in *Montana the Magazine of Western History,* a publication of the Montana Historical Society, Helena, Montana.

Library of Congress Cataloging in Publication Data

Johnson, Dorothy M.
    When you and I were young, Whitefish.

    1. Johnson, Dorothy M.   2. Whitefish (Mont.) — Social
life and customs.   3. Whitefish (Mont.) — Biography.
I. Title.
F739.W45J637   1982   978.6'82   82-14090
ISBN 0-87842-149-1

DEDICATION

This book is dedicated to

MARGUERITE COLE MOOMAW

My companion-at-arms in the Gallic Wars. Shoulder to shoulder, we fought Julius Caesar and the Roman Legions in Whitefish High School, Anno Domini MCMIXX-MCMXX.

Credits

Portions of this book appeared in slightly different form in *Montana the Magazine of Western History,* from Autumn 1973 through Summer 1976 and are used with the gracious permission of William L. Lang, Editor. Some early dates and facts were gleaned from the book, *From Stump Town to Ski Town,* by Betty Shafer and Mable Engelter, Whitefish Library Association, 1973.

My special thanks to Evelyn Stacey Schneider, Marguerite Cole Moomaw, Art and Mable Engelter, Ella Saurey Neitzling, Ralph Stacey, Roy Duff, Dick Adams, and the Montana Historical Society. Thanks and apologies to several helpful persons whose names I'll remember when it's too late to include them here.

Introduction

In the summer of 1973, when I was editor of *Montana the Magazine of Western History,* a manuscript came from Dorothy Johnson. It was her remembrances of working part-time as a telephone operator in her hometown of Whitefish during summer vacations from high school and college. The era: the late 1920s. It was hilarious, but it was also the stuff of history even though not the footnoted, heavily documented (and often dull) material one usually expects to cross the editorial desk of a journal of history.

I knew about Dorothy Johnson, of course. The magazine, published by the Montana Historical Society in Helena, had printed a number of articles by her both before and during my stint in the editor's chair. All her articles had been highly readable and written with wit and sparkle, for that is her style. But they concerned many subjects, some of them deadly serious, such as Kid Curry, the flour famine in Virginia City, a series on Fred Whiteside's courageous exposure of Montana capitol and senatorial graft, some great articles based on the journals of a young son of Wilbur F. Sanders, and the agonizing letters of a man named Frank Kirkaldie who took years trying to make enough money so he could bring his wife and family to join him in Montana.

Now came something different: an article in which Dorothy Johnson herself figured prominently. I recall that I read it first and then passed it around to colleagues, all of whom found it delightful but some of whom questioned its place in a journal such as *Montana*. It was published in the Autumn issue, 1973, under the title *Number Please: True Confessions of a Teen-age "Central."* Response was almost immediate from delighted readers, many of whom carried substantial scholarly credentials.

Although this kind of response, and acceptance, would have pleased any editor, this one was by now so "hooked" on the kind of social and personal history Dorothy Johnson offered that *every new manuscript envelope which came from Missoula was eagerly opened, read, and promptly planned for the next issue. It did not matter, indeed, that as other segments came, they were not necessarily in sequence. Who cared? They were all beautifully written, they were hilariously funny, and yet all contained verities such as patriotism, hard work and striving, family fealty, thrift and neighborliness — and yes, history. Eventually, we published a total of ten segments.

If there had ever been any doubts as to the suitability of this material for a journal of history, they were dispelled in

1978, when I retired as editor of the magazine. In a section of reminiscences about my tenure, published in the autumn issue of that year, John C. Ewers, distinguished Indian ethnologist at the Smithsonian, had this to say: "I have found Dorothy Johnson's recollections of her girlhood in Whitefish back in the '20s nothing less than delightful. Dorothy is of my generation. I noted that she was wearing a fringed cloth imitation of an Indian dress about the same time I was playing Indian in Western Pennsylvania in a make-believe Indian suit of the same material and a band of upright chicken feathers round my head. That was long before Dorothy dreamed of A Man Called Horse or I met a real Blackfoot Indian."

It is little wonder, then, that this writer was overjoyed when the word came that Mountain Press of Missoula had cleared the way for book publication of some of these gems, augmented by others which have more recently come from Dorothy Johnson's inspired typewriter on which the best of muses obviously still sit. As in the days of 1973 through 1976, I can't wait for the mail to come from Missoula.

Vivian A. Paladin
Helena, Montana

Books by
Dorothy M. Johnson

Western Fiction

Beulah Bunny Tells All

Indian Country
(also published as *A Man Called Horse*)

The Hanging Tree

Flame on the Frontier

Buffalo Woman

All the Buffalo Returning

Western Nonfiction

Famous Lawmen of the Old West

Some Went West

Warrior for a Lost Nation, A Biography of Sitting Bull

Montana
(in States of the Nation Series)

Western Badmen

The Bloody Bozeman

When You and I Were Young, Whitefish

About Greece

Greece: Wonderland of the Past and Present

Farewell to Troy

Witch Princess

Humorous History

The Bedside Book of Bastards
(with R.T. Turner)

Contents

New World Of Wonders....1

The Games We Played....6

The Real Pioneers....12

The Painful Path To Larnin'....19

Bringing In The Cash....28

The Fallen Women....42

Fun In The Great Outdoors — or Was It?....47

The Foreigners....64

A King Of Parable....75

Some Inside Dope On City Hall....77

The Preacher Kept A Cow....83

Confessions Of A Telephone Girl....96

Shorty Gammel, Funny-Man....109

World Before Radio....120

The Glacier Obsession...142

What To Do With Snow....157

New World
of Wonders

SOON AFTER THE BEGINNING OF TIME — in March of 1913, to be precise — my parents unloaded me and some suitcases from a passenger train at Whitefish, Montana. I was too sleepy to care. I was seven years old and it was night and there was snow on the ground.

Thus we arrived in my home town. I've lived in several places since and don't live in Whitefish now, but it is still my home town. Everybody ought to have one.

Officially, the frontier was long gone, but Whitefish was a child of the late frontier, still being hacked out of the woods. We were kids together. I was a nice little girl. The town was a sturdy, brawling, mannerless brat that took years to civilize.

The Methodist minister, an old friend of my folks back in Iowa, met us at the depot, and we stayed at the parsonage until we found a house. When my folks took me to see it, I was enchanted. There were mountains all around this town; there were big tree stumps in it and millions of what I called Christmas trees. They had needles instead of leaves, and they stayed green. Those in town were jackpines, up to six feet tall, grown up after one of that area's frequent forest fires. I saw an old bird's nest.

Back at Rainbow Falls, where we had been living, there was rolling prairie, and to see a tree we used to walk half a mile on Sundays to a clump of cottonwoods. Rainbow, seven miles from Great Falls, Montana, was a small settlement of people who worked on the dam the Montana Power Company was building. Before that we lived in Great Falls; before that, in St. Paul, and before that, in Iowa.

It has long embarrassed me that I was born in Iowa. That's a perfectly good place to come from; my mother was born there, too, and so were many other admirable people. But for a person living in Montana, having old roots in the state carries prestige. I am expected to have been born here, instead of in a little town called McGregor on the Mississippi River.

Whitefish — I fell in love with it. My father, in poor health, going into a new job, must have been very hopeful and relieved. My mother, like any uprooted housewife of her time, adjusted and remained homesick for twenty years.

The house my parents bought cost $750; the purchase included two additional building lots. We had three rooms. We had lived in much worse places. At Rainbow, drinking water in barrels had to be hauled seven miles by wagon. Here it was right in the front yard! There was a tall tap out there. Several neighbors who lived farther out had to carry

2

water in buckets from our place. Now and then in winter the tap froze, and my mother scurried around with teakettles of boiling water to thaw it out.

Everybody in Whitefish put up with what they had and hoped for better things. Someone was always building a house or a shack or a privy, or adding on to a house or a shack, or digging a cellar, or something.

That is the test of a frontier town: everybody is still hopeful. Things will be better tomorrow, or anyway right after payday.

In Rainbow, we had had the delight of unlimited electricity, free. The Company made the stuff right there and could afford to give away a little. We even had an electric iron. The electric lines hadn't yet reached our house in Whitefish — way out in the Riverside Addition, five blocks from the center of town — but my parents had of course brought the tried-and-true oil lamps and lantern and the flatirons, to be heated on the kitchen range and set, between swipes, on an old Sears, Roebuck catalogue. The odor of slightly scorched paper still wafts me back to that place, that time, to complete snug protection. It is the smell of home.

Our house, unlike many, was painted on the outside, papered on the inside with fashionable dark reds and greens that swallowed up the lamplight. We had three rooms: front room, bedroom and kitchen.

Later, my folks built on a room called "the shed," which became the kitchen except in cold weather. Rooms weren't specialized. Where the range was, there was the kitchen. With no plumbing, the water supply was wherever one chose to keep the pail and the dipper.

Many people said bucket instead of pail. My childhood was full of confusion about different words with the same meaning, like sack and bag; draw, gulch, and ravine for the depression we called a hollow. Whitefish people came from all over, bringing their own peculiarities of speech. We didn't use the word privy. We said *closet*.

The first school house had a big one for boys and another big one for girls, well separated. We asked the teacher, "Please may I go out?" But a sewer system was being installed in the center of town, and when the new school opened the next fall, we asked, "Please may I go to the basement?" How nice in bad weather! The new school had central heating, too, and radiators that clanged in a friendly fashion.

Downtown (or uptown, as some people figured it) there were wide plank sidewalks. Elsewhere there were only muddy paths.

For grownups, especially women, Whitefish was not idyllic, but for kids it was paradise. Nobody cared what we did to the jackpines, the old logs, the big old tree stumps, the wild roses. We could chop and whittle, cut down a dozen jackpines to make a tepee or a play house. All that had to go sometime. Nobody had to mow a lawn. There weren't any lawns.

Our family went on a fascinating journey on July 4 of our first year there. My father rented a horse and a light rig from the livery stable and drove us eight miles to Columbia Falls to visit some old friends who used to live in Iowa. They had two little boys. That was the first time I was allowed to light my own firecrackers, and my mother was visibly worried.

Also for the first time I was at the base of very big mountains, and with prairie memories still strong, I thought they would fall on me. I still have nightmares about mountains tumbling down on me, but I don't thrive

4

where there are none.

But I am unhappy with no mountains in sight. They protect me from whatever is out there.

Some people in the new town who came from the prairie hated the mountains, which choked and imprisoned them. These unfortunates missed the vast sunshine and the constant wind. Whitefish, in the Rockies, has gray days, and when the wind blows, a storm is coming.

Whitefish has cold nights even in summer. My father was warned that he couldn't raise sweet corn, tomatoes or cucumbers. This challenged him. He had been a market gardener ("truck farmer" in western language) so of course he could raise a little of the same crops he had once grown in abundance. But those plants froze.

Still, it was pleasant to live in a place where a blanket was needed even on summer nights. Everyone adjusted.

The Games
We Played

PART OF MY CHILDHOOD seems now like a glorious, endless summer of running and yelling through tall grass and weeds under big white clouds like whipped cream, riding in a vast blue sky.

There must have been days like that, but as soon as school was out that first year I was put to bed with measles — for the third time. That was before the doctors decided you could have measles only once. When I began to get better, my mother let me look into a mirror. The red and purple swollen horror there caused me to scream and fight.

I was getting back to normal and sitting up, well wrapped, in the darkened front room when the Cooke boys came to call with their mother's permission. Dean was about my age; Billy was a year younger. My mother said I could come out to play in a few days.

Even then, I didn't do much leaping or shouting. I walked rather carefully, seeing dimly through blue glasses. A year or two later I got real glasses.

Sometime in there, we ran and yelled and chopped old rotting logs and saw the wonders in weeds as they grow and go to seed. We snatched at garter snakes and chased gophers and chewed up all sorts of vegetation that didn't kill us. We reveled in dandelions, braided their stems into limp, smelly crowns of gold, blew away the seeds when their yellow hair turned white.

Once my mother, glancing out at masses of blooming dandelions, murmured, "The field of the cloth of gold." Years later I read in a history book about the meeting of a king of France and a king of England in a gaudy pageantry so glittering that the place was called The Field of the Cloth of Gold. Until I read that, I assumed my mother had made up the pretty name.

Dean and Billy and I, still close to the unkempt ground, went over it by inches. We gave names to weeds. I wonder what "wild coffee" really is. "Little cheeses" tasted pretty good.

Once a warning reached my father and Mr. Cooke that, walking to work through knee-high weeds, they had better stick to the trail (we, from Iowa, called it a path) because at the north end of the block a whole incubator full of spoiled eggs had been dumped. A man wouldn't want to step on rotten eggs, would he?

No, but children would. There was an endless treasure of eggs for us to seek out in the tall grass and weeds. Never mind if some were smashed and icky. We found dozens not even cracked.

With screams of delight we gathered them, squabbled over them, pitched them mightily at old tree stumps. What

7

a glorious, stinking splatter! Nobody stopped us. They were nobody's eggs, broken on nobody's tree stumps — we were performing a public service, although we didn't realize it.

What we understood was that we were committing harmless destruction, utterly free, savage and triumphant.

We and our clothing required frowning maternal attention afterward, but that egg throwing experience did something good for us. Maybe it let out some little devils.

And that is a good thing about the frontier.

I read somewhere that in some foreign land, the exotic natives made cloth by beating tree bark, so I pounded faithfully on two-inch-thick bark on an old dead stump, but no metamorphosis was apparent. The people in New Guinea and Fiji still make tapa cloth (I bought some in both places a long time later), but the trees they use don't grow in the Rocky Mountains.

After the Devall family moved into the neighborhood, Henry and Lawrency (and Claudie if he could catch up) enlarged our gang, so we branched out into grander projects, chiefly warfare.

Very little equipment is required for a child with any imagination, and that we had. All kids wore big straw shade hats in summer. Turn the hat up in back and you were a farmer — but what's dramatic about that? We had never heard of the conflicts between nesters and cattlemen. Turn the hat up in front, and behold! a cowboy. We never saw cowboys except in the movies.

A lassoo (we called it) was made of a piece of old clothesline. Whittle a pistol from a thin slat off a banana crate, and what more did you need?

A couple of feathers picked up in the chicken yard and stuck into a headband made a warlike Indian. The juice of wild Oregon grapes was red war paint. My face still hurts when I remember myself, the conquering chief, getting that war paint scrubbed off at home.

A bow was made from a sarvisberry branch. I know, I know — that should be spelled serviceberry, but we didn't know it then, nobody pronounced it that way then and I still think "service" berry is prissy. So we made sarvisberry bows and whittled arrows from banana crates from Mr. Cooke's grocery store. All of us could whittle.

It was the fault of my Uncle Alfred in St. Paul that I became a tomboy. Aunt Mattie was away, and he innocently bought me a boy's Indian suit for Christmas. It had pants. Little girls did not dress like little boys, but I wore out that Indian suit, or outgrew it. I had to fight my way, too. I learned where my solar plexus was when a fist connected with it. Everybody has a solar plexus — how nice to know! Nobody hit for the face. I took a lot of jeering about being Four Eyes, because of glasses.

And so the lovely summers went on forever until the dreadful day when one of the Cooke boys said, "You can't play — you're a squaw!" I trudged home in tears. The snake had entered Eden.

We didn't have playground equipment at school; we didn't need it. For a few years there was a vacant lot, still wild. Little girls could bend down a sarvisberry branch for a door and have an imaginary house. Boys tried to sneak across the street to watch Mr. Parent shoe horses. They were not supposed to bother him. I must have sneaked too, because I remember that wonderful blacksmith shop vividly.

Boys played ball if they had a ball. Girls jumped rope if they had a rope. As we grew, a time came when boys sometimes jumped rope with us, to prove they could, not

9

admitting they liked to be around girls. We turned the rope Pepper and Red Hot Pepper for especially exuberant boys until they got their big feet tangled and went down laughing.

All through the grades we played Statues at recess. One kid swings another around fast by the hand, then lets go. The one who was swung reels a few paces, then freezes into some strange pose, the funnier the better. It must look accidental, but it's not.

All this could be called supervised play, in that an eagle-eyed teacher or two had to stand guard over the swirl of activities and herd the panting bunch back in, marching in a silent double column, as soon as the bell rang. Nobody told us what to play, though, or how to play it. The games and the rules, if any, were traditional; children learned them from other children.

Of course we played games like Hide and Go Seek, but I never quite got the hang of that one. I liked to yell "Olly olly otsin free!" so I yelled it early when I was It, although it was supposed to be a last resort. Those strange words — I asked my mother what they meant.

"All that's out's in free," she explained. She knew just about everything.

The game of Wishing everyone could play, and nobody else needed to know. Sometimes it was the same as Hoping. Hope deferred maketh the heart sick.

Wish I had a bicycle...coaster wagon...pony...new shoes...a million dollars.

Wish I had a red hair-ribbon...blue dress...yellow-haired doll...a million dollars.

Wish Annabell would let me take her to the movies...go for a walk in the moonlight...marry me...wish I had a million dollars.

10

Wish I was pretty with curly hair so Jack would notice me...escort me to church...go walking in the moonlight.

Wish we could move into a decent house before winter, with the baby due in December.

Wish I could stop drinking.

Wish I'd never been born. Wish I'd listened to my folks. Wish I could die.

Wish this day would last forever.

A game of Wish I Could Buy was played with a big mail-order catalog. The whole world's wonders were pictured therein. Every home had a catalog, more thumbed and worn than the family Bible. Hundreds of people older than I was dreamily filled in order blanks, added prices and shipping charges and then, with a sigh, mailed the order in the kitchen stove.

The Real Pioneers

WHITEFISH IS ON THE BURLINGTON NORTHERN Railroad, but when we went there it was the Great Northern. Few people called it that if they were mad about something the railroad did. They blamed everything (except possibly the climate) on "Jim Hill," because it was James J. Hill's railroad, and it's more satisfying to hate a distant ogre than a faceless corporation.

Kalispell, county seat of Flathead County, is sixteen miles south; it had been Jim Hill's division point until he decided to move part of his main line to a less dangerous route through that part of the Rockies. For his new division point, with roundhouse, switch yards, repair facilities and headquarters for a lot of employees, he chose Whitefish, where there was plenty of timber, plenty of water, and

12

already a small, rough settlement of real pioneers. We gave Jim Hill due credit for wisdom in making that change but refused to love him as a founding father. The move left Kalispell depressed and bitter, but it's still bigger and is still the county seat. When I was in high school we had a school yell that really rubbed it in: "Whitefish on the main line! Kalispell on the branch line! Rah rah rah!"

The change was made officially in October 1904, when the last engines from Kalispell moved to the booming little settlement where Whitefish Lake (seven miles long) empties into Whitefish River.

Long before that, Indians had camped there. Arrowheads are still found; it was a kind of factory for projectile points. I remember an old legend of a battle between two tribes on the lake ice when the snow ran red with blood. After the Indians came a few trappers, rootless mountain men. Then came the real pioneers, the footloose, serious fellows who could live off the country while developing it. I went to school with their children.

These men built cabins and took up homesteads in the woods before the country was surveyed. They saw the riches: timber all over the place and water — a network of rivers and two lakes — to transport logs to market in the southern part of the valley, which was opening up. When there was a need for lumber for local building, someone built a sawmill. A couple of small general stores set up business. A few men brought their wives.

And lo! after the railroad came, there was a town, still growing and booming when we got there. The first census, made by C. A. Mathews in March, 1905, counted a population of 950. Mr. Mathews is one of my happy memories; a nice, white-haired gentleman who ran an ice-cream parlor. He could make a fifteen-cent ice-cream sundae

13

with so many elegant flourishes that the expenditure was worth while. He even gave flourishes to putting together a five-cent ice-cream cone. For poetry of motion, for formalized ballet steps with swoops and sweeps of the arms, for grandeur of service, he could have given lessons to tail-coated waiters serving crepes Suzette flaming blue with lighted brandy in an expensive foreign restaurant. I used to play dolls with Mr. Mathews' granddaughters, Doris and Gladys Blume.

A month after his census, the 217 eligible voters (no women — heaven forbid!) voted on whether to incorporate the town. You can imagine the arguments that must have raged: "We need law enforcement, we need local laws, we need a water system and a fire department, we need streets!" versus "But my God, man, we can't afford the taxes! We'll all go broke!"

When the ballots were counted, 153 hot-heads were for government and taxes while 64 conservatives were staunchly opposed. So Whitefish became an incorporated town in Montana, and at the end of that year an infant daughter was born to Mr. and Mrs. Lester E. Johnson at their farm home near McGregor, Iowa, with a woman M.D. officiating — all those years ago, if you can believe it. The Johnsons and Whitefish didn't meet until March of 1913.

A bunch of real pioneers were still around — Bakers, Hutchinsons, Monks, Skyleses, Rupperts, Staceys, Cookes — raising families and with landmarks named for them. A very few of the tough, once fiddle-footed old trailblazers were there, living almost like hermits, not happy to have civilization on their doorsteps but too stubborn to move although not yet too old.

I remember being invited unenthusiastically into the

cabin of one of them with a couple of other kids when we asked for directions to a trail we hadn't been able to find. His great pride was the row of big lard pails hanging inside from the ridgepole. Those pails were full of bear grease, he told us. He had shot the bears and rendered out the grease, and he maintained it was better for cooking, especially pie crust, than lard from any hawg that ever lived.

I remember Dad Lewis fondly. He was a packer and guide for hunters who could afford to pay for their fun. Once when I was backpacking with a girl friend we came upon his camp; he had a customer, and they were traveling with horses, which meant they could live like lords in the wilderness.

Dad Lewis invited us to supper. He made dough-gods, also known as bannocks. Really, they're simple — in theory. Just baking-powder biscuit dough (made from scratch — nobody had invented Bisquick) and fried in bacon grease over a campfire. Ambrosia in the wilderness, that's what — when Dad Lewis made them.

My friend and I followed him and his customer for several days but of course at a slow pace, being on foot. When we came to one of his cold camps, we spent the night there, because he had the secret of making a really good bed out of boughs or swamp weeds or whatever was handy. The beds we made always had sharp ends of something sticking into our ribs. More than once we slept in Dad Lewis's bed. He was miles ahead every time.

He let it be known that he had hunted buffalo on the plains and, later, men in the Philippines during the Spanish-American War. He took part in the Oklahoma land rush. That was in between, in 1893. He told someone he once had a wife but she left him, and so did various partners, because they couldn't get along with him. That

15

doesn't match my recollection of him as a polite, pleasant man who made heavenly dough-gods and invited us to supper.

Old Joe Bush was another hermit-type leftover. I didn't know him well enough to speak to, and anyway he hung around saloons but I didn't. His name wasn't Joe Bush, it was Rudolph Werner; Werner Peak is named for him. According to material on file in the Whitefish Public Library, he once wrote that he was born May 18, 1854; he didn't say where, but people said he was German, and he was unpopular during World War I. He said he served with General George Crook during the Sioux War, and took part in the Battle of the Rosebud June 17, 1876, thereby missing the Custer disaster at the Little Big Horn eight days later. He also fought in the Battle of Slim Buttes, Dakota Territory, in September of the same year.

As a Whitefish pioneer he trapped and traded furs and grew old, and in 1934 he ended it all by taking strychnine poison. His brief final note began, "There is nobody to blame for this but myself but I can't stand it any longer." Maybe the men who knew him best knew what he couldn't stand. Maybe life itself was too much for him after eighty years, a lot of them living alone in the woods.

Among the disasters that struck Whitefish before we arrived were some terrible forest fires and that dedicated anti-sin hellcat, Carrie Nation. Her visit and the very worst forest fire both occurred in 1910. Both Carrie Nation and the Great Fire of 1910 made history. The Great Fire devastated a lot of Idaho and western Montana. Carrie raised hell all over the country. She didn't stay long in Whitefish.

She was violently opposed to liquor, saloons, tobacco, foreign foods, skirts of what she considered improper

16

length and barroom art. She favored women's suffrage; her support plus her disposition probably delayed it for years. Even the national organizations in favor of prohibition and votes for women didn't like her. Her trade mark was a hatchet, with which she chopped up bars. In Whitefish she didn't march into any saloons and chop up things — she was there less than 24 hours — but she did a big business selling souvenir hatchet pins and booklets telling the story of her life.

She started making her presence and displeasure known as soon as she got off the train. The ladies of the local W.C.T.U. had invited her and reserved a room at the Cadillac Hotel for her to rest in; a delegation of ladies met her and took her there. When she found the hotel had a bar (hotels always did), she tore into the ladies something awful for expecting her to rest in that den of iniquity. She took the owner apart, too. He fled, but the escorting ladies couldn't. They hustled her over to the Methodist parsonage, which definitely did not have a bar. She insulted people all the way over there, rested until early evening and then surged out to the red light district to lecture the girls on sin.

By this time she had everybody so mad that it looked as if there might be no audience at all for her speech at the Methodist Church, but 70 persons did attend — some of them unwillingly, no doubt, but lured by the argument, "How many famous speakers ever come to Whitefish?"

Afterward a delegation was glad to escort her back to the depot to be sure the old witch got on the train. She slapped one fresh guy's cigarette out of his mouth on the way, and a man who had been drinking hit her across the face with his hat. Her escort partly muffled their cheers, but another fellow took her side. That was an innocent, gallant mis-

17

take. On the other hand, he must have been drunk — would a sane, sober stranger get into a fight defending that old battle axe? She boarded her train, but both fighters were arrested. Next day one was fined $10 and the other was floated out of town. ("Getting a floater" from the police judge was the euphemism used in those days for banishment.)

Both Carrie Nation and the fire, which kept people scared to death for five months but did not burn the town itself, left scars. It was a good fifty years before the burn scars on the south half of Lion Mountain, west of town, healed over so the mountain was the same shade of dark green from one end to the other. By that time, almost everybody had forgotten the violent Carrie Nation, who died in 1911, a year after she failed to reform Whitefish.

The Painful Path
to Larnin'

Readin' and 'ritin' and 'rithmetic
Taught to the tune of a hickory stick...

NOTHING WAS TAUGHT TO THE TUNE of a hickory stick in Whitefish because hickory didn't grow around there. Parents and teachers made do without it. For small children, mothers plucked a small branch from a sarvisberry bush, stripped the twigs, and applied it to little legs while the culprit screamed, "I'll never do it again" and meant it.

Switching was one step up from spanking, which was disgraceful to any child over four. Another sign of increasing maturity and responsibility was that for saying forbidden words one's mouth was washed out with soap and water. There are two words that I have never used a second time in my whole life. The first time, I didn't know

19

what they meant. My mother didn't inform me, either, but when I think of them, I can taste Ivory soap. Harsh parents used Fels-Naphtha.

At school, children encountered a variety of punishments. On my first day in school, in March, the teacher scared the wits out of me. I was in second grade. The same teacher had first grade, too. She hauled a first-grade boy up to the front of the room and beat him with a wooden pointer.

In case you don't recognize that word, a pointer was a slim, stiff wooden wand about a yard long, used for pointing at A, B, C on the blackboard or, in later grades, at Montenegro or Baluchistan on maps. What ever became of them?

Later that day the same teacher jerked another boy out of his seat and beat *him* lustily. She scowled her fury.

The first boy took it in silence, infuriating her further. He proved he didn't give a damn. The second one howled like a phonograph record. This proved *he* didn't give a damn. Both had had practice in insolence. Hi there, Carroll. Hi there, Earl.

My folks had a real struggle persuading me to go to school the next day. I had resolved to grow up ignorant. In a few weeks of first grade in Great Falls I had been afraid of the teacher, who never smiled. After that, my mother taught me for two hours a day because at Rainbow there were no other children and no school.

The wicked little first-grade boys continued in their sins through high school and were beaten accordingly. They were not born to be hanged. They became exemplary citizens like the rest of us.

Corporal punishment was meted out according to the size of the offender. Through the third grade, the teacher

20

could handle bad kids. In the fourth a couple of boys were broader and more muscular than she was; they had been living on ranches far from schools. For them she called the janitor, in case wrestling might be required. He used a short piece of rubber hose.

Small sins were whispering to a friend, throwing spit-wads or, heaven forbid, laughing. Punishment was standing out in the cloakroom with the coats and overshoes, contemplating one's sins in solitude for fifteen minutes.

Chewing gum was very bad. Eating candy was worse. Just chewing nothing was plain insolence. These stirred teachers to wrath; so did talking without raising one's hand for permission, and sassing back — oh, my! Repetitions of these constituted a felony and earned the rubber hose.

Another punishment wasn't physical but was bad. For some misdeeds one stayed after school for half an hour. Teachers had to stay anyway. They could keep an eye on a couple of small sinners while grading papers. The worst part of this punishment was the need to explain the delayed arrival when the child got home. Parents were always on the teacher's side.

At our house, I graduated from the little switch to a short leather strap. My father had prudently saved it when he sold the farm in Iowa. The strap was earned when I went to play with some other little girl for half an hour and forgot to watch the clock, scaring my mother to distraction. Or the strap might be used when I was lazy about chores like feeding and watering the chickens and carrying in stove wood and then whined about it.

We all had a commandment that Moses didn't mention: Thou shalt obey without pouting at those set in authority over thee.

If a Whitefish child were whipped or even slapped by a

teacher now, his parents would sue the schoolboard and yell about his civil rights. It was not a member of the disciplined generation who burned down the big high school gymnasium and all the school band instruments in 1977 just for kicks.

So much for the hickory stick. We learned reading. Our school readers stressed literature of by-gone days. Authors were men with beards, except Edgar Allan Poe had a little mustache.

Literature was *Hiawatha* and *Evangeline* and "Build ye more stately mansions, O my soul," and inspiring stories like "The Great Stone Face." Years later I took a hard look at that face in its native New Hampshire but couldn't see anything inspiring about it. We had a big monkey face on a mountain east of town that was much more interesting. It's not there any more. Tree growth has hidden it.

I was very fond of reading, but the old poets and preachy prose writers tended to use language like the Bible or Shakespeare, with thee and thou and strange verb forms that we never heard in real life.

Hail to thee, blithe spirit! Bird thou never wert... Shelly was crazy about a skylark. We loved our meadowlarks but never talked to them that way.

I was going to be a poet, so I tried to get the hang of this language, but it didn't fit northwestern Montana.

We read aloud, prodded by the teacher, and memorized chunks of poetry. Anything a child might want to read for pleasure wasn't literature. Neither was anything published in the twentieth century. Our books were pretty old.

In the eighth grade we had Physiology, which was not, believe me, sex education. The only thing I remember from that course was that you shouldn't build your privy where it would drain into your well.

Maybe the Whitefish schools didn't turn out the world's best spellers, but our teachers certainly tried, clear through high school. Many years later, when I was teaching magazine courses at the University of Montana, one of my colleagues in the School of Journalism brought me a composition written by his little girl, who was in the fourth grade. I noticed eleven words spelled wrong on one page.

There was no grade, but the teached had written EX-CELLANT.

The worried father and I agreed that, since the teacher couldn't spell, either, she should confine herself to GOOD.

He sighed. "It's no use to complain to the teacher. Spelling errors don't count any more. It's the new educational philosophy. Correct the child's spelling and you may block her creativity."

My opinion is that letting a kid spell wrong does not help him be creative. Creative people find complete freedom within the bounds of discipline.

We learned punctuation, too. We learned grammar. And I studied grammar some more in college.

But when I taught at my alma mater, I had juniors and seniors who had not been exposed to English grammar at all. Only when they studied a foreign language did they find out their own language had any. I couldn't tell them when the passive voice comes in handy because they didn't know there was one. Of course there isn't always, so I lectured on transitive and intransitive verbs. In the School of Journalism, careful use of language matters.

Back to Whitefish: in the grades, we wrote compositions as part of reading. In high school the course was English, and we wrote themes, at least one every two weeks. The teacher read them carefully and pointed out our mistakes.

23

Handwriting was drilled into us painfully. The system was called the Palmer Method. One girl actually liked it and practiced in her spare time, hoping to earn some kind of certificate. Even our teachers didn't write Palmer Method except when they were showing off at the blackboard. We all wrote, however. We didn't print. I learned that in science courses in college.

Arithmetic taught us some things we never needed to know, like how many rolls of wall paper to buy for a room of certain dimensions, deducting for windows, and how much plaster for a room. This required addition, subtraction, and multiplication, maybe division too. There were no pocket calculators.

Eighth-grade arithmetic was a killer. We did partial payments. Buy a house for $3,250 (a real dream house!) at six per cent compounded, payable monthly over ten years, and how much is each payment? Make one mistake and all those pages of calculations are wrong from there on. After we found that the teacher, a tired old lady, simply threw our papers in the waste basket and guessed at a grade, we didn't worry very much. In real life, people just consulted the bank when applying for a mortgage. There was no point in arguing with the bank's printed tables.

In high school, algebra and geometry were required, maybe to strengthen our characters. I also took advanced algebra but can't for the life of me remember why.

Our high school was small, so we didn't have many courses to choose among. I took typing and shorthand and earned my living with them for some years afterward. And "general science" and chemistry and biology and Latin and some history courses. My mother confided that she had liked ancient history because it was sort of vague about dates.

24

Art was not taught, but we were exposed to it. Every room had one or two pictures on the wall, in shades of gray or brown. Some were patriotic, like the portrait of Abraham Lincoln or Washington Crossing the Delaware. That one worried us. Every child in Whitefish knew better than to stand up in a boat.

Some pictures portrayed great writers, but they all looked alike with those beards. And some were reproductions of great paintings like The Angelus or the Blue Boy. It was a surprise to us when we grew up and found out that the great paintings were not originally in shades of brown. They had real colors!

Grade school and high school were all in one building, added onto as tax income permitted. Domestic science had its own frame house, perhaps because a dozen girls learning to cook rice can become distractingly noisy. A gymnasium was added after a few years — at first, only for the boys' basketball team.

The coach was Harry L. Hayden, truly a man of many talents. He was superintendent of schools, high school principal and a teacher of almost anything. He taught my geometry class. At recess, he kept swarming children off the newly planted lawn. (Even nice girls like me tended to edge onto the struggling grass when playing a hot game of mumbledy-peg.)

There was no school band. A music teacher downtown, who also sold instruments, set up a boys' band that entertained loudly. There was a glee club, beloved by those who could carry a tune. Naturally, I wasn't in it.

There was no football. There weren't enough boys in the whole high school. Few boys went to high school. Big boys could go to work and be useful citizens.

Most girls went to high school mainly to kill time until

25

they got married. Jobs for girls were very, very few.

I wonder what became of Bert. He was bigger than the other boys in the eighth grade. His voice had changed, and he wore long pants. Most of the other boys were at the stage where they yearned for long pants as a sign of maturity, but their parents said the old knickerbockers would do for a while yet. Bert was an earnest student. He paid attention. He didn't read aloud very well (he was not alone) but he tried hard.

Bert was laughingly patient, like an indulgent young uncle, when four or five cooking-class girls shrieked around him, offering him biscuits they had just baked.

He was sadly patient when the teacher nagged him for being tardy almost every day. Tardiness was a sin. He took her scoldings, explaining that his father made him late; he had chores to do. Then why, she demanded, didn't he get up earlier?

"Pa would just find more chores for me to do," he answered.

The teacher could accept no excuse for being tardy so often. She kept nagging.

Bert, determined to finish the eighth grade, held his ground between Pa and the teacher all that year. He didn't go on to high school.

The teacher didn't pity him. I did, and I still do.

Like some primitive societies, we had our rites of passage, marking the change from little kids to big kids. Ours came mostly with the change from eighth grade to high school.

Girls yearned to do their hair up and let their skirts down. Boys yearned to wear long pants instead of knickers. Girls whined and coaxed their mothers. Boys growled and argued with their fathers. But making the change

26

depended on one's age, and how tall we grew was beyond our control.

Besides, prudent parents did not let a boy graduate from knickers to long pants until he wore out the knickers or his younger brother grew into them. A boy's suit cost money. Girls' clothes were usually made at home and cost less.

Girls wore high-topped shoes, with buttons in grade school, but laced when we got bigger. A well-dressed girl had no knots showing where her laces had broken and been tied together. (For dress-up we wore strapped patent-leather slippers with flat heels, called Mary Janes.) High laced shoes were said to keep a girl's ankles slim, but what good was that when nobody saw them?

Boys, after they began to notice girls, brushed their hair straight back and applied grease to keep it there. On a blackboard at the back of a college classroom in my freshman year there was a row of spots where young men, leaning back, had rested their heads. Above it some wit had written: THE GLORY THAT WAS GREASE.

Girls of my high school generation, when we were allowed to put away our hair ribbons and do our hair up, wore cootie cages over the ears. These were puffs, either carefully snarled or filled with small store-bought pads of fiber that tended to fall out before the day was over. We called them rats, but they looked more like mice. In the back we made a kind of knob or small bun.

This fashion was followed by one known as the bushel basket; various versions of it have come and gone since. The hair was puffed all over, with small rats at the sides and a big one across the top, and sooner or later something was pretty sure to fall out.

Now our rites of passage are long forgotten. Both boys and girls are born into long pants, faded, frayed and patched, depending on fickle fashion, and you can't tell one sex from another by either clothing or length of hair. Of course beards and mustaches help in identification.

Probably we looked funny, but we tried, according to our lights, to look nice.

Bringing In The Cash

THE RAW NEW TOWN swarmed with money-hungry children who were willing to do almost anything to make an honest nickel. The trouble was that just about everything you could do was part of your normal chores and you didn't get paid for it. Like filling the woodbox or lugging in a bucket of water while your mother admonished automatically, "Now don't hurt your back," or splitting kindling while she warned, "Now don't chop your foot." Or feeding the chickens, carrying out the swill bucket, washing dishes, picking potato bugs and shoveling snow.

You couldn't earn money by mowing lawns, because nobody had one; there was enough work for grownups to do just hacking the town out of the woods without planting and tending grass. A couple of yards near us had a good stand of clover, which the householders were willing to have me cut with a hand sickle and take home in a gunny sack, to be spread out and dried for winter feed for our chickens. Pour a kettle of boiling water over a bucket of dry clover and you get a nice salad for hungry hens, but this paid off in chicken and dumplings, not in cash.

There simply was no dependable source of income for children. Running errands (most people didn't need telephones — they had kids) was a thing they were supposed to do, free for their relatives and just possibly paid — a nickel from the prudent, a dime from the reckless — when done for neighbors.

This wasn't a businesslike arrangement, though, like the one I have now with a boy down the street. When he mows my lawn with my power mower, we both know how much he's going to get for it. When a kid ran an errand in Whitefish, there was normally no previous discussion of remuneration. When he got back, all sweaty and eager, and was offered money, he was supposed to pretend surprise, even shock if possible, and refuse but not very convincingly. Then the lady who had commissioned the expedition insisted with persuasive charm and finally he let her press the coin into his hand and both of them thanked each other several times. This was the ideal; it didn't always hold. Sometimes he only got a cookie.

A couple of errands that I ran for my mother ended in disaster. Right on the doorstep of a lady to whom I was delivering a lard pail containing a dozen beautiful eggs, I stumbled and dropped the whole works. It took her quite a while and several cookies to calm me down and mop my tears.

Another time, taking something to a Mrs. Soward, I was attacked by ducks. In the summer any child's bare legs were thoroughly mosquito bitten and well scratched, with plenty of big scabs in various degrees of healing. Mrs.

29

Soward's ducks found my scabs very tasty, and I shrieked bloody murder, up to my knees in child-eating ducks. I never went back to her house again. Our chickens sometimes pecked at my scabs in a thoughtful, investigative way, but ducks bite.

In reading a bound volume of *St. Nicholas Magazine*, I came upon the word *allowance*. The concept was attractive. I researched this pretty thoroughly. According to stories in *St. Nicholas*, an allowance was money your parents gave you regularly just because you were there. You didn't do anything to earn it. This struck me as an admirable idea. No child I knew in Whitefish received an allowance, not even the scions of locomotive engineers, those lords of creation who were paid a very great deal of money by the Great Northern.

Assuming that an allowance was something my parents had simply overlooked, I brought up the subject, suggesting that any small amount would be acceptable as long as it was steady. My father, looking startled, asked where I had heard of such a thing, and I said, "In *St. Nicholas*." He and my mother stared at each other. *St. Nicholas* was a children's magazine of good repute. They hadn't suspected that it was subversive.

After I explained gladly about allowances (it was seldom that I knew more about something than my parents did), they got the idea across tactfully that maybe some children in some places received allowances but no such outlandish custom was going to be introduced in Whitefish, anyway not at our house. This was back in the days when parents and children could still communicate.

My copies of *St. Nicholas* were dated the same year I was and were bound as a big, heavy book. Once I asked how come we had these old magazines around, and my

30

mother replied briefly that when I was born my father rushed out and bought a year's subscription. Some new fathers rally 'round with a catcher's mitt. Mine subscribed to a magazine. I see the philosophy behind it this way: He realized that, small as I was, I wouldn't be getting around much for a while and he thought I would appreciate having something to read in bed.

A copy came faithfully each month, but I wasn't as precocious as he expected, so he had them bound to keep them from being scattered. I didn't learn to read *St. Nicholas* until a few years later. It was a good magazine, but some of the ideas in it didn't fit life in Whitefish very well.

There was a time when I thought everybody was good and kind and honest like my folks. Disillusionment rocked me at about age eight. There was an ad somewhere about how you could give away beautiful pictures to the neighbors and get a set of bluebird china absolutely free. It wouldn't cost you a cent. You wouldn't get a cent either, but I visualized myself playing Lady Bountiful and presenting my mother with a set of china all painted with bluebirds of happiness. So I mailed the coupon.

The deal turned out to be not precisely as advertised. Before you could give a grateful neighbor lady one of the beautiful, artistic pictures, you had to sell her several packages of garden seeds. These included some species that wouldn't mature in our cold climate under any circumstances. Nobody wanted those garden seeds. Although art standards were not very high in Whitefish, the pictures were so garish that only one potential customer was attracted, and even she wouldn't be caught dead trying to raise cabbage and tomatoes from seed.

So I sadly gave up on the bluebird china. Time passed,

31

and a letter came from the company, a letter calculated to scare the wits out of a hardened criminal. They threatened to sue me — me, mind you, who had hardly a blot on my record aside from having to stand in the hall a couple of times at school for whispering. My mother helped me pack up and return the seeds and the pictures, and she may have written them a letter. No more was heard about the proposed lawsuit.

Not everybody a child might try to do business with was crooked. *Youth's Companion* practically promised the earth, and it was ready to deliver. For them you simply sold subscriptions. *Youth's Companion* was a weekly publication for children, with highly moral stories and puzzles and such. For so many subscriptions and a little cash money, they offered the equivalent of ivory and apes and peacocks.

My best customer was our dentist, Dr. Spinney, who either had an awful lot of young nieces and nephews or just enjoyed listening over and over to the sales pitch of a little girl who lisped. I found him fascinating, too. He had a human skull in his office and he let me borrow it. I took it to school and treasured it at home until my parents got tired of seeing it in the dining room and persuaded me to return it.

Thanks to Dr. Spinney and other nice people who were willing to pay for an uplifting magazine, I got a heavy gray sweater that lasted for years, six silver-plated fruit knives for my aunt (who had no great need for six fruit knives, but they made· an impressive Christmas present), a magic lantern that threw an enlarged image of picture postcards on a sheet, and other marvelous things.

There was more. If you totaled up a whole lot of orders, *Youth's Companion* paid a bonus in honest-to-goodness

32

gold, coin of the realm. They sent me a gold piece worth $2.50, very tiny, and a slightly bigger one worth $5.00. Wow! My mother reminded me that, however pleasant it was to handle these lovely coins, they would grow into even more money if deposited in my savings account. So I took them to the bank. But when I dropped in there one day, just wanting to see that my gold coins were all right, the bank didn't know where they were!

The bank explained that yes, they had my money; they would give it back any time I wanted it, plus four percent; they would even give it to me in gold. But they had not, as I expected, put those particular coins on a little shelf somewhere. They had mixed them in with their ordinary money, and nobody knew where they were! I have never really trusted a bank since then. And I'll bet the entire staff of the First National went home that day with a splitting headache.

The bank's high-handed way of handling my money no doubt saved me from developing into a miser hovering with wild witch giggles over a pile of gold. Those two tiny coins were all the gold I ever had. A passbook simply doesn't have the same mad magic.

Although the term "baby sitting" had not entered our lanuage, the custom was already a part of our culture. It was called "keeping care of kids." Some little girls made as much as two bits an evening at this if the parents of the kids they were keeping care of stayed out really late. But they were girls who had learned the technique at home and practiced it on their younger siblings. I had no siblings and no preparation, so the first time I tried it was the last.

There were two kids to keep care of. The parents left no instructions but sailed out merrily and stayed out until one in the morning. The baby slept soundly as he was sup-

33

posed to, but the older child demanded "kigh-go" and wouldn't go to sleep without it. I didn't know what a kigh-go was. Tiger, maybe? There wasn't a tiger in sight, so I offered him a small stuffed horse. It didn't fool him for a minute. He kept yelling for kigh-go; he wept, he demanded, he implored. Although I frantically offered him everything but the heavier furniture, he was not appeased. He cried himself to sleep and I cowered in a corner until his folks came home.

Queried about kigh-go, his mother replied casually, "Oh, yes, he always wants a cracker — they're right there in the kitchen." I left the money-making possibilities of keeping care of kids to girls who were better qualified. I preferred to deal with persons who spoke the same language I did.

The Big Tin Can Cleanup provided a bonanza for children. The infant town of Whitefish got along for several years quite nicely (although not neatly) without garbage disposal until some sharp-eyed radical reformer noticed that the toddling baby was up to its knees in trash, mainly old tin cans.

This was before "biodegradable," before "ecology." Shucks, ecology was what everyone was trying to get rid of. There was so much ecology that there wasn't room for people to build houses. A million young jackpines were in the way, and hundreds of big tree stumps, most of them black with charcoal from one or another of the forest fires that had nearly wiped out the town a few years before. The blackened stumps were dandy for kids to climb around on and a cause for bitter complaint by mothers as they lugged out the clothes boiler, washboard and laundry soap.

The wild beasts that were part of the ecology had to go, too. Mrs. Jefferson, who lived across the alley from us, had a run-in with a mountain lion a few months before we moved to Whitefish in 1913, and when we met her she was still mad. This horrid, snarling creature, as big as she was and a lot more dangerous, came right up on her back porch. I don't remember what she said she did about it. She was little, but she wouldn't put up with much nonsense. She probably took after the big cat with a double-bitted axe.

Anyway, ecology had to go. The town needed room to grow. Meanwhile it produced a certain amount of trash. There was no waste paper; people used that for starting the fire. Bones you could toss out and some dog would be grateful, or several dogs would co-operate on the remains of a butchered deer. There was much excitement when some bones were dug up that seemed to be human hands, but they were traced to a finicky-neat hunter who had buried the feet of a bear.

Coffee grounds, egg shells and potato peelings were biodegradable: nature took care of them. (My mother saved potato peelings and boiled them up with a handful of wheat. The mess smelled awful, but our chickens liked it.) Tin cans, however, only accumulated and did not decay. And there was a limit to how many you could use for storing nails or growing geraniums on the window sill.

By the time I was nine or ten, the tin cans were causing official concern. All the back yards and a few front ones had a terminal moraine of rusty cans. Vacant lots had great piles of them. When anyone bought a house, it was customary to toss all the cans that came with it onto the next empty lot. The first Big Money I ever earned was 15 cents for doing that. The job took several days. Of course, for pay like that, it should.

The city council, composed of men able to solve problems they had never faced before, solved two problems at once. The other one, besides the tin cans, was gullies. Whitefish streets are level now, but they used to go up and down. Sidewalks, where there were any, were made of wood. Across the gullies they were built on rickety wooden trestles that swayed when walked upon. Some streets were almost level but swampy, and during the spring thaw those sidewalks floated.

The city fathers conceived the idea of putting the tin cans in the gullies, thus getting rid of two nuisances. Tin cans and gullies were just made for each other. The problem of transporting the cans was easily solved. There were all those kids, not doing much except playing cowboys-and-Indians. The city government made a handsome offer. For every 100 cans a kid delivered to an assigned gully, he would be paid five cents.

A juvenile gold rush took place. We were surrounded by treasure. We went mad. We staked out claims in the neighbors' back yards and worked them with energy and dedication. There was some claim jumping, of course. The little Franco boys tried to jump a claim of mine in Mrs. Coffman's yard, but she was vigilant and chased them off.

The only equipment needed was an old gunny sack. A child with a coaster wagon could haul two sacks of cans at a time and make considerable speed until one of the sacks fell off. I burst into tears when Jimmie and Frankie Franco rattled past me, jeering. We who had no wheels had to drag our filled gunny sacks, and that wore holes in them so the cans leaked out. On the other hand, a boy with a wagon had to have his brother along to help fight off hijackers, so they divided the money and I suppose we all came out even. Prosperity depended on industry.

The tin-can cleanup was conducted with great dignity in

36

the higher echelons. Whitefish had two police officers, Ben Holter and George Tayler, each on duty twelve hours every day. Both of them waited at the selected gully. Both wore stern mustaches; they were pretty stern men. Mr. Holter, I heard, once brought in four wanted men at the end of an empty gun; they thought he still had one shot left and were taking no chances. Mr. Tayler, I overheard my father say, had killed a man by mistake, shooting at his legs just as he jumped down a cutbank, and still felt terrible about it.

They radiated authority. They did not wear uniforms. They wore ordinary dark clothing, always a vest to pin the badge on, and Stetsons with moderately wide, severely flat brims. Those men were, believe me, The Law.

Children trotted to the gully, dirty and breathless and half scared, handed over a sack full of cans, and watched a lawman solemnly count them as he tossed them over the brink. There had better be an entire 100 in the sack, too, or the nickel would be withheld until the guilty child scrounged more cans and delivered them with proper expressions of repentance. Not being able to count as high as 100 was no excuse. The assumption was that if you brought less than 100 cans you intended to cheat. One boy tried to outsmart the vigilant lawmen with a mere 79 cans, and we were all embarrassed.

Mr. Tayler was my father's best friend. I called him Uncle George. He was just as dignified counting cans while an anxious child looked on as when he strode the streets looking for trouble or sang "Bringing in the Sheaves" in the congregation at the Methodist Church.

Every kid who tried to cheat got caught at it and was chastened with a stern look and a few words from Uncle George or Mr. Holter. No doubt several budding criminals

37

were jarred back to the straight and narrow by that experience. Crime did not pay, but a full count of rusty cans did. When you had passed inspection, the majesty of the law put a nickel in your dirty hand and gave back your empty sack. Virtuous and rich, you lit out to get more cans. (The improvident lit out for the candy counter at Crum's Grocery Store.)

And ah, the glory of it when your third or fourth sack was accepted by one of those splendid officers *without counting!* Your integrity had been established. You were numbered among the righteous, and when the roll was called up yonder, you'd be there. Your strength was the strength of ten because your heart was pure. From then on, you tended to put in a couple of extra cans for good measure. I remember worrying: Did a very small flat sardine can really balance a big tomato can in the scale of justice? I decided to count the sardine can as different but equal, but sometimes I still wonder.

There was nothing aesthetic about digging dirty, rusted, stinking old cans out of a pile of garbage and counting them into a dirty gunny sack. Cans had sharp edges. Sometimes they had rain water in them, and nasty little crawling creatures. But if this unsanitary aspect bothered any parents, their children went ahead anyway. Nobody got blood poison.

It takes a lot of cans to fill a big gully, and a lot of cans was just what Whitefish had. We filled those gullies, and somebody hauled dirt to cover the mess. When the wooden trestles quietly decayed, they were replaced with concrete sidewalks — a reckless extravagance, many taxpayers felt.

Where the gullies used to be, there are level streets constructed so long ago that most people who live in Whitefish now assume they were always there, like the

Rocky Mountains. Among the buildings based on a solid foundation of rusty cans, the enthusiastic labor of money-hungry children, and the ingenuity of an early city council, are two churches so long established that their mortgages are all paid off.

Tears come to my eyes, even now, at the very thought of horseradish. For a time — too long a time, God wot — I was the Horseradish Queen of Whitefish. I never sought the honor and I abdicated as soon as possible; probably the title is still up for grabs. Someone gave us some horse-radish roots, and my mother peeled and ground them and mixed in some vinegar and said it was very good with hash. I never could see it, myself. She threw out the odd bits and pieces and they grew like crazy right outside the back door. That's how we happened to have horseradish.

My mother, an ingenious woman, learned that there was a market for ground horseradish around town, so she put me in the business of selling it. I didn't mind digging the roots and complained only a little about peeling or scrap-ing them, but grinding them in the food chopper was awful. I wept buckets, and we usually ended with her doing the grinding and weeping. She also stirred in the vinegar and measured the mixture into odds and ends of small glasses, on each of which she set a price. I peddled the stuff and got to keep all the money. Looking back, I see this as a one-sided arrangement all in my favor, but it seemed reasonable enough then.

The town was full of crazy people who thought the product was great. Hori's Cafe bought it a quart at a time, for half a dollar and please return the Mason jar. A vision of so much money, glimpsed dimly beyond the curtain of my tears, was all that kept me going. I went out of business when we ran out of small containers. We never did run out of horseradish roots.

Some money-grubbing children rushed out and spent their income at once. I put mine in the bank, not always voluntarily. But it was understood that I had to go to college when the time came, and that would be expensive. After my father died, in the week before my tenth birthday and his forty-fifth, earning and saving became even more important.

The following spring, however, I almost blew five dollars. Forrest Forcum rode a girl's bicycle that he hated, and when he got one of the right gender he was willing to sell the old one cheap. I bought it on a trial basis but never did get past the falling-off stage in trying to tame it. My mother decided to spend the summer with her sister in St. Paul, attending business college, and I thought it might be nice to have some money to spend in the big city, so I returned Forky's bicycle and he, under pressure, returned my five dollars. When we went back to Whitefish in the fall, I still had $4.85.

Two years later I used my savings to end World War I. It had been going on for quite a while. Food shortages and economies we could put up with, and colors that ran because no more dyes came from Germany, but Uncle George was Over There, and I was worried. He wrote awfully good letters. The first time I ever saw the word *morale,* it was in his handwriting.

There were Liberty Bonds to win the war with. You could buy one for fifty dollars — and clip coupons off it for the interest. I consulted my mother: was this investment really safe?

"If we can't trust the United States Government, we can't trust anything," she replied. So I counted my assets; cash on hand and the nickel-and-dime savings of a twelve-year lifetime came to $47.10. I decided to shoot the works. My mother felt that I was a fairly good credit risk and lent me the necessary $2.90 without interest to make up the total.

What happened after that is history. The Allied Armies took heart on the Western Front. The Kaiser, informed by German Intelligence that the little Johnson girl in Whitefish, Montana, had bought a Liberty Bond, yelled, *"Mein Gott! alles kaput!"* and heaved his spiked helmet through a window of his palace. The Armistice was signed November 11, 1918. And Uncle George came back and married Miss Huntington, who had been my fourth-grade teacher.

The Fallen Women

OUR TOWN HAD, OF COURSE, its red-light district, which nice little girls didn't need to know anything about. Even now I don't know where ours was in the early days; it was restricted in area, no doubt, and in some spot handy for railroad men and lumberjacks.

I know the police kept an eye on it, because years later, when I worked for the City Clerk and Attorney, I used to kill time by reading the very early records of the town. I came upon some lists of female names with fines paid on what looked like a regular basis — the frontier equivalent of licenses to do business. The public treasury always needed money.

The only soiled dove I knew by sight was Julia. She bought a house in our block for her sole occupancy and retired. The ancient Greeks had a term for this: She "hung up her mirror.'' The neighbors did not drop in to welcome her. They ignored Julia, except that boys passing by snickered knowingly. Julia ignored the neighbors. She was just a stout, well-corseted, aging single woman who had an occasional circumspect male caller — some lonely old friend who came through the alley to her back door late at night.

Evelyn Stacey Schneider told me years later that a good woman in town taught old Julia to read and write, after she was retired and had time to learn. For a respectable woman to do this was an act of real charity, because being in the same room with a professional fallen woman must have made her shudder.

Julia was smart and learned fast. She already knew arithmetic. She was very good indeed with numbers, especially those with dollar signs in front of them. She had saved money and invested it wisely, and when she hung up her mirror, she could well afford it.

Back in the early days, before younger free-lances ruined the business for professionals, soiled doves usually stayed away from downtown. But their money was as legal currency as anybody's, and their custom was important to some stores. (Groceries and meat could be ordered by telephone or messenger and delivered by wagon, like everyone else's.) One married couple, active in our church, ran a small specialty store. When one of the girls came in to look around, the proprietors dropped everything and everybody to attend to her need for silk stockings or whatever. They dropped me one day — maybe I was looking at hair ribbons for a birthday present — and I walked out, offended.

But the girls didn't have much money. The madams did. Trust the excutive type to get the gravy! Following an unwritten law, the madams did not sally forth in person and shock the people by flouncing along Central Avenue to visit the stores. They sent messages, describing what they'd like to look at. They shopped like royalty. The Queen of England doesn't paw through merchandise in shops. Purveyors are glad to send stuff over on approval.

Evelyn's father, Simon Stacey, ran a jewelry store. He was a godly man, a member of our church, father of small children. Buyers of jewelry were not abundant in Whitefish, but a store that sold and repaired clocks and watches was a necessity of civilization in a railroad town. The Great Northern sometimes had wrecks, but they were not due to somebody's watch being wrong. Train conductors, locomotive engineers and firemen (who had to substitute for engineers in emergencies), brakemen and even switchmen bought the best watches available and had them checked for accuracy every so often. For this, they went to Stacey's.

Sales of other items weren't tremendous. An engagement ring with a teensy diamond, a wedding band, some silver-plated knives and forks, a sterling baby spoon with curled handle, gold lockets that would hold a tiny picture or a lock of hair, watch fobs, stick pins, cuff links — these were gifts for grand occasions.

But the general population had no money to waste on jewelry. The madams did. Besides, diamonds were a girl's best friend, because she might have to leave town in too big a hurry to pull her stake out of the bank.

Occasionally Simon Stacey received a note suggesting, for example, "I would like to look over some diamond rings," or bracelets or necklaces or brooches.

So he packed up a nice tray of whatever it was, wrapped it, and walked the several blocks from his place of business

44

to the customer's, hoping he wouldn't be seen. There, at her leisure, the madam examined the merchandise, discussed prices and bought what no honest woman in town could afford.

On one occasion, Mr. Stacey was impressed by the genteel manners of his hostess, by the good taste of her parlor and by the just-right elegance of her dress. After she made her selection and paid for it, she said, "I understand, Mr. Stacey, that you came originally from England?"

"I did," he agreed. "Some years ago."

"It happens," said she, "that I have some real English plum pudding. Would you care to take tea with me?"

He certainly would. Drinking tea and eating real English plum pudding with a fallen woman wouldn't endanger his immortal soul, would it? So she called in Beulah or whoever the maid was and ordered tea. Simon Stacey's eyes almost popped out. The tea itself was English, the elegant tea set was Spode, the plum pudding was perfect and the conversation impeccably correct.

They parted politely. Simon Stacey had enjoyed his afternoon on the edge of sin and his conscience was clear, but this was not a story he cared to tell his wife or his mother-in-law. So he confided in his older brother, Tom.

Tom was a bachelor who didn't talk much. He was an upright citizen like Simon, like him a model of rectitude, but sterner and, I remember, rather gruff. (Later he became police judge.)

Simon's story about his adventure fascinated Tom, because he liked English plum pudding, too, and he wasn't about to send to Fortnum and Mason's in London for it. He suggested, "Don't you sometimes do repair work for that woman, on a watch or restringing a necklace or something? Next time you have a delivery to make there, let me take it. Before the plum pudding runs out."

A day came soon when Simon had a repaired mantel clock to be returned. It was an expensive clock.

"All you have to do is be sure it keeps running after you put it on the mantel," he warned. "It must be absolutely level. Be careful of it, and good luck with the plum pudding."

Off went Tom in his best suit, with the neatly wrapped clock under his arm. Visions of plum pudding danced in his head. He knocked on the door and it swung wide open — to reveal one of the girls, naked as the day she was born.

Alas, poor Tom! He took one horrified look and was so shocked that he forgot all about plum pudding and making sure the repaired clock set on an absolutely level surface. He simply dropped it on the nearest chair and ran as fast as he could back to the respectable part of town where women didn't answer the door unless they had all their clothes on.

Fun in
the Great Outdoors—
Or Was It?

OUTDOOR RECREATION had two great advantages when I was growing up: it was handy, and it was cheap. Whitefish lacked a lot of things, but it certainly had outdoors, right up close.

We didn't need a permit or very much equipment to go camping. Those compact, comfortable machines for roughing it that people call campers hadn't been invented. Campers were all people. Roads were few and awful, but we didn't need them for camping. There were (sometimes) trails. The trick was to get on the right trail and then not lose it.

The first camping trip in which I participated came close to disaster. At age seven or eight, I was the youngest member of the party and the least worried.

My father, Lester Johnson, had been a farmer in Iowa. He didn't pretend to be a woodsman. The other man in

47

the group was our neighbor, Jack Jefferson, an express messenger who hailed from Minot, North Dakota. He was our trail boss. He knew where we were going, and he was in charge of the pack mare.

There were seven females in the party — eight if you count the pack mare; she caused all our trouble. The others were my mother, me, Mrs. Jefferson (a tiny woman slightly handicapped by a broken arm in a sling), and four teen-age girls: Grace and Ethel Van Dyke, Mrs. Jefferson's sister, Clara, and Ella Saurey. Ella was about fourteen when all this happened. A few years ago she cleared up for me some details that I had forgotten.

All the females in the party (except, of course, the pack mare) wore bib overalls. Ladies didn't normally wear men's clothes in those days, but long skirts were no good for climbing over down timber in the woods.

What we went for, Ella remembered, was huckleberries. That figures. They were there, they were free, and they made good pies. And we had to have some sound reason for the expedition; in those days, people didn't like to admit that they did anything just for fun.

We went in what should have been relative comfort. We didn't have to back-pack because we had that old mare, with Mr. Jefferson in charge. She carried our bedding and all our utensils, such as coffee pot, axe, frying pan and eating tools, and all our grub except a slab of bacon that one of the girls had in a fishing creel.

See the jaunty campers swinging along toward the mountains north of town. After three or four miles they are not so jaunty any more. They have reached the foothills and are plodding, not swinging. See them slap mosquitoes, ha ha. See them sweat, so that one by one they take off their sweaters and let Mr. Jefferson put them on top of the horse. This they'll regret.

Some of the jolly hikers are learning a thing or two, like when to climb over logs and when to duck under down timber. The others knew already. They are resting more often now. They are thinking that it will be nice to stop and build a fire in front of the old cabin Mr. Jefferson knows about and lay out all those blankets and have a good supper and go to bed early. Isn't it nice to have everything on the pack horse?

But where is the pack horse? For that matter, where is Mr. Jefferson? Why are the hikers suddenly excited? Are they lost? No, they are not lost; they have arrived at the cabin. But Mr. Jefferson and the horse are missing, with all the comforts of home.

Now what are they going to do? Why, yell so Mr. Jefferson will know where they are. Yell, hikers, yell. No answer. Just when did they lose Mr. Jefferson, anyway? Probably back yonder when they ducked under a fallen tree but he had to lead the horse around it. And he must have got onto a different trail and where is he now? Yell, yell, yell — calmly, of course.

And who just tripped over a root and rolled down the trail? Why, that was Mrs. Jefferson being calm with her broken arm in a sling.

See the dauntless campers making the best of it in the wilderness. They may be inexperienced, but they are not stupid. They have matches and jackknives. So they build a nice fire outside the cabin and everybody scurries around collecting firewood. Lots of firewood. They scurry some more to bring back great armfuls of sweet-smelling giant ferns to make a nice thick bed in the cabin — but without any blankets. Every now and then they all yell for Mr. Jefferson.

49

They use their pocketknives to sharpen sticks and to slice that slab of bacon. They cook the bacon on the sticks and let the grease drip on their wet shoes. After it is dark they hear a couple of pistol shots far away and decide that this is a message from Mr. Jefferson, indicating that he is thinking of them.

Meanwhile, in another part of the forest, see the pack horse. See Mr. Jefferson. Why is Mr. Jefferson mad? Because the place where he is spending the night does not have running water or any other kind. He has blankets and coats and plenty of grub and a six-shooter with ammunition, but he cannot have a drink of plain ordinary water. Neither can the old white mare, but never mind her. To hell with her. He speaks to her in a most unfriendly way as he opens a can of evaporated milk. It will never take the place of water. Then he hobbles the pack horse so she can't get away, and he goes to bed but he cannot sleep very well. Come daylight he will load up the horse and catch up with the rest of his party.

The horse doesn't sleep very well either. She suspects a bear in the neighborhood, and she craves friendly company. Since she cannot crawl under the blankets with Mr. Jefferson, she gets as close to the campfire as possible. Sometime during the night when Mr. Jefferson is dozing, the horse becomes convinced that the bear is close by and yearning for nice fresh horse meat. So in spite of the hobbles she heads back toward town as fast as she can go.

Mr. Jefferson awakes in a hurry. He tries to catch the horse, but she can see better in the dark than he can. Alas, poor Mr. Jefferson! His campers are in one place, he and the contents of the pack are in another place, and the old white mare is a rapidly moving object somewhere else in the forest primeval. Somehow he has to get all these things

50

together in one place before the other members of the party starve — and he doesn't know for sure whether they ever reached the cabin he had told them about. He has a big, bad problem in logistics. And he can't begin to solve it until there's enough daylight so he can start back down the trail after that homesick horse.

Along toward noon, up at the old cabin, see the brave campers, still with their chins up, tired of bacon straight, not happy to observe that there is practically no bacon left to be tired of. Hear Mr. Jefferson, down the trail, fire his revolver to let them know he is coming. Hear the campers yell and cheer. See Mr. Jefferson trudging up the trail leading the retrieved pack horse. See Mrs. Jefferson, being very calm, run toward him, trip over a root, and roll down the slope again with her broken arm in a sling. See everybody happy, happy, happy!

That is all I remember about the camping trip. In my memory, the story ends with the grand reunion. Ella remembers that we went on to another cabin, below the old Micho mine, the second night, and stayed out a third night and did get huckleberries.

Now I realize that they must all have been afraid and worried, but they never let me guess. I found the situation very interesting, but that was all. I don't even remember being cold during the night. I learned that bacon, which I had disliked until that time, is perfectly delicious. True, everybody scavenged around and built up a huge pile of firewood, and someone kept a big fire going outside the cabin all night, but they must have told me that was so Mr. Jefferson could find us. Nobody said a word about needing a fire to scare off bears.

At my age nothing awful had ever happened to me; my parents kept bad things away. I had never been afraid of anything or anybody except my first and second grade teachers. Since that blissful, carefree time of my life I have become one of the world's great worriers, with good reason. But there was a lovely time when I was very young and able to take it for granted that every story has a happy ending.

The older girls in the party weren't so lucky. They had lived long enough to learn that bad things can happen even to the nicest people. But however close they may have been to tears or hysteria, they said nothing to suggest to a little girl that we might be in an awful fix. Ella, Clara, Grace and Ethel, I salute you.

Another camping trip included my parents and me and Ella Saurey. We traveled by train, disembarked with our belongings where a signpost said Gary and camped very near the railroad track. This may have been another huckleberry expedition. (Some people like huckleberries better than I do.)

What I remember about this camp is my mother's growing horror at the housekeeping habits of a fisherman who was camped there alone. He never washed his frying pan or his plate. For breakfast he fried bacon; at noon he fried trout in the bacon grease, and again for supper. The next day he did the same thing. The idea of cooking bacon after fish gave my mother the collywobbles. Ah, well, he was a free spirit who just didn't like to wash dishes.

The big problem about camping was to get the equipment to a suitable place without having to backpack very far. A boat was fine if you wanted to camp on the shore of Whitefish Lake. (Of course first you had to get your stuff from your house to the boat.)

Once with two other teen-agers I had permission to stay out as long as the grub lasted. We made it stretch by shooting two pine squirrels for meat; we had a few sad potatoes and enough saved-up bacon grease to fry the squirrels and make gravy thickened with pancake flour.

A pine squirrel, skinned and dressed out, is pitifully small. If you have a cavity in a back tooth you can mislay your whole meat ration. Next morning we voted unanimously to go home, unable to face a diet of pancake flour and spring water. We had used up all the bacon grease and scared off all the squirrels.

Real camping, with no transportation, was harder. When you omit all the food you can't carry on your back because it is too bulky (bread, dry cereal, salad materials), too heavy (potatoes and all other fresh vegetables, fresh fruits, canned food, anything in glass), too fragile (eggs), or too spoilable (milk, butter, fresh meat), what have you got left? Nothing fit to eat, that's what.

The more I think about it, the more I wonder why anybody bothered to answer the call of the wild. Convenience foods — dried, freeze-dried and instant — hadn't been invented. There was something that purported to be dried milk; mixed with water, it tasted awful. There were dried eggs, expensive and hard to get and also awful.

A day's menu came out about this way:

Breakfast: Bacon, pancakes fried in grease, no syrup. Or cornmeal mush with prunes or raisins cooked in it, and that peculiar-tasting reconstituted milk.

Lunch: Cold pancakes and bacon or cold cornmeal mush. Because if you stop long enough to unpack and build a fire, you'll never get where you're planning to go, and the slower you travel the longer you'll be subsisting on this ghastly grub.

Supper: Fried trout if you're lucky, but don't count on it. Bacon, scrambled eggs, bannocks, gravy (made of bacon

53

grease, that queer milk, and flour), very plain cake if you're ambitious. Bannocks are baking powder biscuits fried instead of baked, and pretty good. Cake mix was far in the future, undreamed of. You made camping cake from scratch, using bacon grease because there was no butter, and powdered eggs and awful dried milk — no flavoring. You baked in a pie tin, using campfire heat reflected from a small square of tin that you carried along for that purpose.

Let's look at the period in the context of anthropological development. Man had learned to use fire; we carried matches in a Prince Albert tin. He had invented the wheel — not that it did any good on narrow mountain trails. He had even invented gunpowder and firearms. But all the things that make camping easy and comfortable now he just hadn't got around to yet.

Among the first things a small child learned were: take along some matches in case you get lost, be sure to put out your campfire thoroughly, and never point a gun at anybody even if you know it's not loaded.

I usually carried a .38 revolver in a holster when hiking or else a .22 repeating rifle, but if you're carrying a pack it's better to have your hands free. Experienced woodsmen chortled about my firearms, advising, "If you meet a bear, throw the gun at him and run."

One time the .38 came in handy even without bears. An equally weary companion and I had arrived at a lake where we intended to camp, but the sound of splashing and cheerful male voices indicated that somebody had got there before us. Flashes of white through the trees indicated that the swimmers were bare. That far from civilization, they should have been safe. I ought to explain that this was about 1924, and both we back-packing girls and the swimming boys would have been greatly embarrassed by a confrontation.

My friend and I yelled at each other, which wasn't necessary because we were only ten feet apart. The swimmers didn't hear us. So I pulled out my trusty hawg laig and fired it into the air to attract their attention and then we yelled at each other again. Our soprano yells came close to paralyzing those fellows. There was dead silence up ahead, then frenzied activity. We sat down, rested our packs against a handy log, and discussed the day's journey loudly in tedious detail. When it seemed prudent to resume our journey, we expressed surprise and delight to find two high school boys from home camped there.

"We were swimming," one of them remarked.

"Ah, yes, your hair's wet," said one of us. "Hey, you're missing one shirt sleeve."

"Yeah," said the one-sleeve camper, blushing, "we got dressed in an awful hurry."

Other times, other customs. My .38 was never needed to throw at a bear, but it came in handy that time to permit swimmers to preserve their dignity with the loss of only one shirt sleeve.

We may call the period B.P. — Before Plastics. There were no handy little transparent plastic bags or jars to carry things in. There were no big sheets of plastic for wrapping wet bathing suits, wet dish towels or wet anything. There were no detergents. You started out with a bar of soap, and if you were lucky you didn't lose it until a couple of days before you got home. This was not only Before Plastics; it was before nylon, transistor radios, cigarette lighters, spray cans, Scotch tape, ballpoint pens and paperback books. When you wanted to pack up after cooking a meal, utensils were too greasy, too smoke-blackened and too hot.

55

The other day, comparing camping then with camping now, I took a look at the packages of freeze-dried food currently available to backpackers. They include pork chops, cottage cheese, tuna salad, shrimp cocktail, beef stroganoff and chocolate cream pie. Shocking, that's what it is. It may taste good, for all I know, but that kind of gourmet coddling won't strengthen anybody's character like cold cornmeal mush. Of course, lots of people don't even want their characters strengthened.

To go camping the easy way, with a vehicle to carry the impedimenta, was sort of cheating. I cheated whenever possible. On one such trip, three of us unloaded in a pleasant natural meadow by a stream, said good-bye to the obliging truck driver, and wrestled up a pup tent that would give a mature Chihuahua screaming claustro-phobia. That night we were all in it, like teaspoons, when some monstrous beast invaded our camp, snorted around and knocked some things over. We were curious, but not curious enough to crawl out and take a look. No bron-tosaurus or sabre-tooth tiger had been reported along the South Fork of the Flathead River, but that didn't prove there weren't any. Maybe the adventurers who had encountered them just never came home and weren't missed.

The beast came the second night, too, and this time it was even madder. Our visitor made loud huffing noises while tearing a dish towel to shreds. It raged and stamped and left footprints, from which we deduced that it was a deer complaining that we were ruining the neighborhood.

The nights there were haunted but the days were en-chanted. I don't remember what my companions did for amusement. I spent the time playing with butterflies. The river — icy and swirling, full of foam and rapids and

56

sucking whirlpools — was some distance from camp. Between the white water and the black wall of the forest was a long, sweet stretch of white sand. I wore a swimsuit but did not venture into that savage water. I just played in the sand and dreamed, and the butterflies found me.

There were millions of them, brown and gold. They alighted on me, wing-quivering, in such hordes that I thought I too might fly. They uncurled their mouths (like tiny, coiled-up hoses) and kissed me delicately and flew away and alighted again to savor this new wonder, the taste of human skin. When I moved, they fluttered, and I chased clouds of them over the white sand, and they settled on me again in silky glory when I stopped and was quiet.

That enchanted beach is lost now, doubly lost. No living being can ever again see that white sand between the river and the forest or invite the kisses of the butterflies. First a forest fire destroyed the place. Then the reservoir behind Hungry Horse Dam flooded it forever. But in my memory it remains as it was, untouched, unhurt by fire or flood or time, and sometimes I go spinning back to it, and the butterflies still dance forever and flutter down to kiss my skin. It is my secret, remembered place where nobody goes but me.

Some of the denizens of the wild used to become remarkably fierce under certain circumstances — if backpackers were really hungry for meat, for instance. Like those two pine squirrels I mentioned earlier. Why, they growled and roared and showed their teeth until we had to unlimber our artillery. We defended ourselves with my .22 rifle, because the four-ten shotgun would have demolished them completely.

On another trip, three separate pairs of back-packers we

met had fresh venison, and all of them maintained that they had fired in self defense. We agreed that a buck deer can get very mean in August, or even a doe if that's what you happen to meet. It was harder to understand when a couple of boys told of being attacked by angry grouse, but no doubt the birds were as vicious as reported.

It used to be illegal to kill porcupines, the theory being that a starving man without a gun could club one to death for food. I don't know what roast porcupine tastes like now that it's legal, but it was pretty good, like pork, the one time I ate some.

The first rule of camping was that it would probably rain, so you ought to have a tent. A pup tent would keep some of the rain off if you had (1) strength enough to carry all that heavy canvas and (2) patience enough to hitch it up when you made camp. It was easier to be optimistic and go to bed thinking it wouldn't rain; when it did, you could pull the thing over you and lie there wishing you'd been smart enough to stay home.

Or you could take a smaller hunk of canvas, a tarpaulin (called a tarpoleon), sometimes known as a shelter half. Half of two recumbent campers was about what it would shelter, and not even that if the wind blew. Canvas was very heavy to carry. Now there are nylon tents, light as a cloud. Ah, me.

In theory, cedar boughs made a fine bed, but a solid protuberance always developed that threatened to perforate your rib cage. For cutting cedar boughs and firewood you needed an axe. If it was big enough to be efficient, it was awfully heavy. A small axe in a leather case hitched to your belt was handy but so ineffective for chopping that you might as well gnaw the wood like a beaver.

Axes haven't changed much, but they're not used so

58

often. Nowadays some back packers take along a one-burner stove for cooking. There's one that weighs only 18 ounces when filled with two hours' worth of fuel. Anyway, firewood is harder to find than it used to be because of continuing wear and tear on campsites. Wood is still needed for an ordinary fire to keep campers warm while they sit around telling lies, but any day now someone will patent an instant fireplace (just add water) with built-in hi-fi and automatic corn popper, all reduced to the size of a deck of cards for easy carrying.

Back to the bed making. On top of the cedar boughs went the blankets. Sleeping bags hadn't been invented. There were huge safety pins to hold blankets in a sack shape after you figured out how to fold them. It's possible that some campers still use blankets, because although down sleeping bags, weighing from two and a half to five pounds, are very nice, they are very expensive. In fact, what it now costs to get a good camping outfit together used to be enough to put a kid through a year of college.

Obviously I was never a dedicated camper or I would not now look back on those experiences with profound relief that they need not be repeated. On the other hand, without those memories I could not now so thoroughly enjoy luxury hotels. How can anyone really appreciate the elegance of cherries Jubilee or French snails with garlic butter who never choked down a lunch of cold bacon and pancakes?

Hiking (without a backpack, and home for supper) was what I really liked — enough to go by myself if there was no prospect of company. If people go hiking now around Whitefish, it's hard to figure out where they go unless they use a car to start out with. The close-by woods have disappeared; any place you might want to walk to is

59

somebody's front lawn. It used to be that all you needed was a direction. After a couple of miles you could pretend nobody had ever been there before unless you came to a deserted cabin. Then you could make up stories about what bad-man-on-the-run had inhabited it.

Old cabins were fascinating. They smelled of pack rats and old socks. There were empty whiskey bottles under the bunks and empty corn-cure bottles all over the floor. I still wonder why the men who lived there temporarily were all subject to sore feet. Maybe because they never washed their socks.

A hike that was a real workout was to Beaver Lake, the other side of Lion Mountain, west of town. There were two ways to get there, but it was about five miles either way. One approach involved balancing on the sides of your feet while picking your way across a long stretch of shale on the far side of the mountain. There was no trail at that spot because the shale kept sliding down the slope, and hikers had to be nimble or they'd go with it.

Once Ruth Dugan and I took swimming suits to Beaver Lake and, after making sure the cabin there was not inhabited, went swimming. There was no beach. It was mucky quicksand with water lilies. So we dived from the shaky little wooden dock and then skinned out of our suits and hung them on handy nails. We were splashing around happily in the utter freedom of skinny dipping when we heard wild laughter from across the lake.

We hastened to get back into our suits and become once more the modest mermaids our mothers thought we were. Picture it for yourself: two desperate damsels trying to put on wet swimming suits under water with nothing to stand on and no way to hang on to the dock for support because we needed both hands to manage the suits. We were

60

competent swimmers, but here were problems we had never encountered before. Treading water was not easy while we tried to thrust our feet through the places where the feet had to go. We struggled and gulped and went under several times, becoming tangled in dangling water lilies.

When we surfaced, gasping, that wild laughter was closer, but we couldn't see any boat. All we could see was a swimming bird that looked something like a duck. Only then did we realize that loons really laugh. We were so shaken that we got dressed at once and headed for home, by wagon road and railroad track.

The Eighth Annual Commencement of Whitefish High School, it says here on the old program I have before me, took place May 18, 1922, with thirteen sweet girl graduates and one lonely boy lined up in glory on the platform at the Masonic Temple. Now it can be told that five of those girls had been lost in the woods the day before, and it was my fault. Or shall we say it was the fault of the four who chose me as guide and trail blazer on the senior hike? I wasn't as smart as we all thought I was.

I chose to take us into the foothills north of town, where I didn't know my way around at all. We plunged doggedly up hill and down, with me telling one fast fib after another about where we were and where we were going, not admitting that we were totally lost. I was mightily relieved when we finally came to a vantage point from which we could see which way Whitefish was.

We did get back all right, but Ruth Diver had such a fearful sunburn that she was utterly miserable while we sat there in the Masonic Temple all decked out in our pastel organdy dresses, and pretended to listen to whatever good advice the commencement speaker gave us. Ruth's dress was pale blue, a spectacular contrast with her sunburn.

Swimming in Whitefish Lake was a big thing — and still is, on a larger scale because it is now a recreation center that draws people from many states and Canada. It was nicer when it didn't seem to belong to anybody.

There was always a problem of where to dress at the city beach. Sometimes there were dressing shacks (and the City Council was criticized for wasting the taxpayers' money) and sometimes there weren't so we hid in the bushes. Bad boys poked holes in the walls of the girls' shack for peeking purposes, but smart girls indignantly plugged them or hung clothes over them.

A few times I dressed at the home of some people on Lakeside Hill, but their neighbors complained on seeing me walk by in my bathing suit. No doubt a twelve-year-old girl child in a swimsuit that came down almost to her knees was just too sexy.

There was never a life guard at the city beach but there were no drownings. There were no little kids floating on inner tubes either. We simply learned to swim, each after his own fashion, and wherever we swam out to we jolly well had to swim back from. Once three of us swam across the bay by easy stages, with considerable floating and back-stroking, ate some nice green apples we found growing on Baker's Point, and swam back. On mature reflection, I don't think this was a good idea.

Years later, swimming in Lake Winnebago in Wisconsin, I found out that kids in that area had teachers and as a result all swam the same way. Some years after that, living in New York City and on a vacation at a summer camp in New Jersey, I ran into a bunch of rules that made me downright mad. City girls liked to have their recreation planned — play volley ball for an hour, do something else

62

for half an hour, swim at a specified time, with every minute supervised. And everybody had to swim the same stroke! We swam that stroke or else stayed in shallow water inside a slimy wooden enclosure.

My swimming is what you might call free style. It gets me there and brings me back, and I never aspired to Olympic competition. No self-reliant daughter of the untrammeled West could put up with such regimentation as that place imposed. I was there for a vacation, not to serve a sentence in a minimum-security prison camp. So on the third day of what was supposed to be two weeks of wholesome outdoor living I told the lady warden I had to get back to the city to consult my doctor. She didn't quite believe that, but she couldn't prove it wasn't true.

I spent the rest of the two weeks in New York, sweaty but free. I'll bet that bossy swimming instructor never swam a bay in Whitefish Lake after eating green apples. Probably she never roasted bacon on a stick, either, or had butterflies come fluttering down to kiss her.

The Foreigners

WE WERE PAROCHIAL IN WHITEFISH. It was so new a town that almost nobody over the age of ten had been born there; we had all traveled to get there from wherever we lived before. But we had always lived in the United States. Foreign travel wasn't even an impossible dream. It was beyond comprehension. And some of course, were foreigners. The fact that they spoke little English embarrassed us.

This was long before high school kids soared blithely off to spend a school term living with a family in, say, Sweden or Scotland and being foreigners. It was even before a lot of grown-up Americans traveled by ship to Europe to fight a war that was supposed to make the world safe for

64

democracy and to discover that the French didn't pronounce the name of their own capital city right — they called it "Paree."

Whitefish did have a handful of young veterans of the War With Spain, men who had fought briefly in the Philippines or Cuba, but that experience had done nothing to contribute to international understanding.

What we did in Whitefish when we encountered foreigners was to avoid them, if possible, after efforts to communicate in the only language we knew broke down.

There were many Japanese in town; we never knew them well because none of them lived near us. Everybody knew M. M. Hori though; he was a big shot businessman who smoked cigars, owned a prosperous truck farm, a hotel and restaurant, and lunched regularly with the bank president and other dignitaries, who nicknamed him "Swede." His pretty wife was known as "the last of the Japanese picture brides," and legend said he had imported her after marrying her picture. He got his start as a houseboy for a rich family in Kalispell, who gave him ten acres of land that he built into a fortune. He was out of our class.

When a new family moved into the two-story log house down by the river, I was pleased because they had a little girl, Mary, about my age — eight — and it would be nice to have a little girl to play with for a change from the little boys with whom the neighborhood was infested. But when I went to see about this, Mary couldn't come out. Her mother needed her. We never did play together, because her mother always needed her, and I'm not aware that Mary ever complained about it. She smiled shyly and went right on doing whatever she was doing. It was useful, necessary, and expected of her.

65

The family's name was Franco, and they came from Italy, which was unimaginably far away. The father's name was Pasquale. Younger than Mary were Jimmie and Frankie and some others. Hard working Mrs. Franco needed more daughters, but she was a steady producer of boy babies. My mother and I called once to see the newest one, about three days old, and Mrs. Franco — who had picked up a little English by that time — boasted that the baby was saying "papa" already. He was sort of purring with his lips. Mrs. Franco loved them all, whether she needed any more or not. Frankie was a trial to her; she once told my mother he was "all same one little devil — one minute lick, next minute run — oh my God!" but she loved him too, even while she chased him so she could swat him a good hard blow.

The Francos were not the first foreigners I ever knew. There had been a Finnish family next door to us in Great Falls, where we lived before — desperately poor people. I remember hearing my father say grimly, "That man could earn five dollars a day as a carpenter if he didn't drink!" and I understood that five dollars a day was untold riches. My father, well educated for his time and in such poor health that he had given up farming in Iowa, was earning forty dollars a month heaving freight at the railroad depot in Great Falls.

One day my mother, weeping, told my father that the Finnish lady was so completely out of food that she didn't even have salt to put into the last of the oatmeal to feed the five children.

I never knew what became of the hungry Finns in Great Falls, who could have been so rich if the father hadn't been a drunkard. But I knew what poor was, from listening to my folks worry about them. We weren't poor; I didn't know until years later that life was hard for my parents in Great Falls. I did understand that something was wrong, because I caught my mother wiping her eyes as she finished making my Christmas present, a new bonnet sewed from scraps for my favorite doll, Bluebell. The bonnet looked very pretty on Bluebell, and both she and I were pleased.

Then things changed for us. My father got a job as timekeeper for the men who worked at the Montana Power Company's Rainbow Dam, and we moved out to Rainbow Falls and lived in a tarpaper-covered shack by the railroad. The few times we went into town we sat on the platform of a railroad handcar operated by the muscle power of two men who pumped a heavy bar that made the wheels move.

At Rainbow, where probably less than a hundred people lived, a surprising number were foreigners, because there were two railroad section crews, one bunch Japanese, the others Greek. The two crews lived separately and worked separately. The Greeks had nothing to do with anyone else, except once when they sent a man to our house on a desperate mission. What he said he wanted was "ingun," and when my mother finally understood that he needed an onion, both of them were pretty well worn out. We didn't know any of the Greeks.

The Japanese were different. They were, no doubt, just as homesick as the Greeks, just as frugal in saving money to send home, but they were friendly. Some of them spoke English well and the rest were learning it. They all had names. (If the Greeks did, we never learned them.)

John Kimura was six feet tall — a giant among his smaller companions. I remember him best because he saved my life once. I was watching the section crew work

67

where the track went through a cut, and I began to play on their handcar. The big two-man handle that propelled it was so heavy that they didn't dream a six-year-old child could work it, but I got the vehicle to inch along and was having great fun.

Then, the men heard a train whistle — the fast mail, not far off around a bend; they were always alert for trains. John Kimura got to me first. He tossed me to safety into the dirt a few feet from the track, grabbed the under side of the handcar with both hands and flipped it over onto its back, and leaped out of the way. The train roared by, and he carried me home in his arms. I have never forgotten the look of horror on his face.

Another of the men, whose name we pronounced Hah-tah, visited our tarpaper shack one or two evenings a week; my father tutored him in political economy.

My mother had two pupils at Rainbow. She had taught country school in Iowa for five years, starting at age sixteen. Now she taught English to the power plant manager's Swedish hired girl, and for two hours a day she taught me, because I had been removed from the first grade in Great Falls. In this brisk intellectual atmosphere I tried to teach our cat to read, but he kept dozing off. So I read anything available; chiefly I recall *Freckles* and *The Girl of the Limberlost,* novels by Gene Stratton Porter. (I never thought of being lonely for other children; I had two imaginary playmates, Alice Syrup and Mabel MacNamara, and we got along fine.)

When we moved to Whitefish, it was no doubt my parents' experiences with foreigners in Rainbow that prompted them to reach out to the Francos, whom most of the neighbors ignored because they were different.

The Francos were by no means poor. They were, in

68

their own eyes, rich and prosperous. They had reached at least the anteroom of paradise. Whitefish was for them the promised land, flowing with milk and honey. All they had to do to enjoy it was to work.

Their ways were not our ways. My mother baked our bread in the oven of a wood-burning range, baker's bread being for bachelors and the families of lazy women. She made three handsome brown loaves at a time, the tops shiny from being rubbed with saved-up butter wrappers. But Mrs. Franco baked up a fifty-pound sack of flour at a time, in round loaves, and her oven was out in the back yard, made of bricks or stones or concrete (I don't clearly remember) and shaped like a beehive.

Once Mr. Franco, who often spoke in praise of his wife's skill, showed my father and me a great pile of new loaves stacked outside the back door, ready to store inside. Grinning happily, he picked one up and beat on it with his fist to show how substantial it was. The crust didn't crack.

"See?" he said, with pardonable pride. "Good bread!"

They must have had help in building that oven, perhaps from some of the other Italian families in town.

Mrs. Franco and little Mary made all the pasta for the household, none of this boughten stuff for them. They knew how it ought to be, and that's the way they made it — tons of it. I was there one time, probably hoping Mary could come out and play, and saw how they did it before they got their magic machine. The dough was mixed (and what a muscle-building job that must have been!) and they rolled it out in thin sheets on the floured table. Then, using an umbrella rib and a couple of expert twists of the wrists, Mary made a long tube of macaroni — anyway it was a tube after a knife deftly cut along the rib and quick hands slid it off and hung it up to dry. Those singly-made tubes of pasta hung all over the house until they were dry — on clotheslines and stair rails and the backs of chairs.

When they got their magic machine, Mr. Franco was so proud that he came up to our house and invited us down to have a look. His wife was a good cook and he believed in giving her the best possible equipment, and in this wonderfully prosperous country he could afford it. The machine, he told us, cost forty dollars, although it wasn't very big.

It was a wonderful timesaver. Just put the dough in a kind of hopper, force it down, turn the handle — and out through holes in the bottom came a whole bunch of endless strands of pasta! No more umbrella rib! And with the magic machine they could be any size, from vermicelli up to big thick tubes. It all depended on a thing inside that governed the size. The Francos were as pleased with that machine as their children probably were with their first Buick.

Even before they attained the luxury of the pasta machine, they reveled in the use of a lot of land that didn't seem to belong to anybody. Anyway, nobody was using it, except that children like me played on it. There were a couple of city blocks of it, with some fire-blackened stumps and old rotting logs and wild roses and wild grasses that grew knee high. From somewhere the Francos imported two goats, a nanny and a billy. Why let all that good grass go to waste? A goat was a more familiar animal to the Francos than a cow and didn't require a huge investment of capital.

Mrs. Franco, with everything else she had to do, was always dragging a goat around at the end of a rope from one good grazing spot to another. She walked fast, whether the goat liked it or not, and as she pulled the balky

70

animal along she looked dreamily contented. Such a good place to live! So many things free! But she cannily kept the goats off some of the grassy places, and when the proper season came, she made hay. Mr. Franco cut it with a scythe, and they put it up in great thick braids. I have never seen braided hay anywhere else but people in Italy may be making it to this day for all I know. Great twisted braids of it hung on the Francos' fence to cure before they put it in a shed for winter feed.

Coal was free, too. There were chunks of it along the railroad track, spilled out of coal cars, just going to waste, and Mr. Franco, that good provider, kept track of its location. Now and then he and his wife walked three or four miles in the cool of the evening carrying empty gunny sacks, into which they carefully dropped the waste coal. When they had a good load, they walked home, with Mr. Franco well ahead and his wife dragging the biggest sackful and both looking triumphant. Such a good country! So many things free!

And some things just being wasted. The Cookes lived near the Francos, and from Mr. Cooke's grocery store emanated a great many wooden boxes; this was before things were shipped in cartons. These apple boxes and such were fine for kindling, and lots of people made temporary furniture from them, but when the pile got too high down at the store Mr. Cooke sent a load of boxes home in his delivery wagon to be burned. Something had to be done with them. There was no city dump. Nobody fretted about polluting the air with smoke. The air was already so full of smoke from forest fires that we had glorious, spectacular sunsets.

Those boxes made grand bonfires for the Cooke boys and their friends, including me. We danced and howled and yelled while the flames leaped and the smoke rolled upward.

The first time Mrs. Franco saw one of these periodic conflagrations she couldn't stand it. She came running and shouting, trying to make us stop throwing boxes on the bonfire. Because of the language barrier, only minimal communication was achieved, but one thing was clear: the dreadful waste of all that wood upset her. Discussion on a higher level than ours (Mr. Cooke talked to Mr. Franco) established the rule that Mrs. Franco could have all the boxes she could use or store in her yard, but the rest of them we could burn because they had to be got out of the way.

Long later, Ralph Stacey told me a story about the Francos' billy goat. Ralph was a very little boy, a couple of blocks from home, when he had his awful adventure. He was with another boy, only a little older, who had a beebee gun, when they saw the billy goat grazing. The other kid took a shot at it with the beebee gun. The billy goat, enraged, charged with his head down. The boy with the toy gun ran and got over a fence. But Ralphie's legs were too short — he couldn't get over the fence, and neither could he run very fast.

So, screaming bloody murder, with the angry goat hard on his heels, he headed for our house.

"And," he told me, "your mother came out and saved me and chased off the billy goat. That was one of the worst experiences of my life. And I wasn't even the one who shot the beebee at him!"

Poor little Ralphie. He was pretty young to start learning how cruel the world can be. He had remembered that terror and injustice for sixty years.

There were several Italian families in town, but none of

72

them lived near the Francos. My parents were as friendly as the landguage barrier would permit. Once the Francos invited us over for supper. They must have fed their children earlier; none of them were at the table. I found the food very strange indeed, and asked for a glass of water with the meal. Mr. Franco thought that was pretty funny, but his wife brought me one.

And then came disaster. With flourishes, Mr. Franco poured a glass of wine — his best, no doubt — for each of my parents. They were strict Prohibitionists. My mother didn't know what the liquid was. My father, more worldly, did. He classed it as the Demon Rum.

It is hard to explain for modern readers how fierce was the hatred of those who fought alcoholic beverages. People addicted to drink had not yet been adjudged "sick." They were just plain sinners. One taste could set a person on the downward path to hell. Methodists were in the forefront of this battle. The miracle at the wedding in Cana, where Christ turned water into wine, was glossed over in our church and Sunday School. It wasn't really wine, but probably plain grape juice, such as we had on Communion Sunday, or else wine was different in New Testament times.

If this were a *Reader's Digest* story, full of sweetness and light and human understanding, my father would have taken a sip of wine just to make Mr. Franco happy. But he didn't. He couldn't. In his youth he had signed the pledge, and he was a man of principle — the kind of principle that used to get people burned at the stake for their beliefs. He pushed back the glass, said, "No, thank you," and left our host completely bewildered.

Let it be said in my father's defense that he didn't preach to Mr. Franco about the evils of drink. He was as courteous as his rigid standards would permit. He knew that foreigners had strange customs.

And let it be said for Mr. Franco that wine was perfectly legal. The Volstead Act, the 18th Amendment, was some years in the future.

That disastrous dinner took place when I was about eight years old. Remembering it still embarrasses me, still makes me pity those two well-meaning men of differing cultures who were trying hard to be friends.

The following summer my father was sick; I can't really remember him when he was well, but now he was very sick, in bed at home, and my mother was caring for him. Uncle George Tayler saw to getting our big garden ploughed and planted. Sometimes he hoed weeds. My mother hoed when my father slept fitfully; it was a chance to get outside. I carried in water and stove wood; those were normal chores for children.

And sometimes Mr. and Mrs. Franco — both of them — came and hilled up our potatoes. They had a big garden of their own. I don't think Mr. Franco worked in it — that was not proper for the family head, who had a wife and children for such tasks. But he and Mrs. Franco toiled in our garden, shoulder to shoulder, to help us in our time of need.

My father died in December. It must have been two weeks later that Mr. and Mrs. Franco came to our house, both crying. They did not, of course, read the paper; they did not talk to the neighbors because of the language barrier — and they had just found out (so late! so shamefully late!) about my father's death.

When they had gone, my mother sobbed, repeating, "I should have thought to tell them! They are such good friends."

A few years later, the Franco family moved to California. They were going to have a vineyard and raise grapes for making wine. And before very long, the making of wine was illegal. I wonder what happened to those fine people. Something good, I hope.

My mother didn't waste much time in crying. But I remember once...

She was reeling after my father's death and facing open-eyed our situation of financial need; she sat at the kitchen table with pencil and paper planning meals. I sat by her with nothing to offer but good will.

Sighing, she said, "Guess I'll have beans."

I asked, "Are beans cheap?" knowing that cheapness was a great virtue.

"Nothing's cheap," she answered, and put her face down on her crossed arms while I hovered anxiously.

Then she stood up, blew her nose, gave me a hug, and went on coping.

Never again did she hint that we had money troubles. We just didn't waste any money. It was understood that what I earned was to be saved for college. We gave each other and our relatives presents for Christmas; we gave each other birthday gifts, and my mother took delight for years in the fact that I didn't know her age. (With a December 30 birthday, it's hard to figure.)

I learned young by example the grace of receiving, of being delighted and never, never disappointed.

Once I broke the rule and loudly pined for something — a package of three tiny bottles of cheap perfume at Mr. Haines's drug store. The price was a quarter. I was about twelve. My mother was embarrassed at the fuss I made; she did not buy the perfume, and on the way home she made a few remarks about little girls who whined.

75

Still, the perfume was under our Christmas tree, "from Santa Claus." I knew that must be Mr. Haines.

Many years later, when we were living in New York and I was juggling two careers (magazine editing as a job full time and writing in spare time) so we were more prosperous, I gave her a real surprise at Christmas. With other gifts, pretty and useful things, I tucked in new one-dollar bills, a few here and a few there, a total of one hundred. Both of us came close to hysterics.

But in the long-ago time, when she was coping, she worked at many jobs to earn a little money. For a while she gathered news items for the weekly *Whitefish Pilot,* the social items that readers in those days wanted.

For this we had a telephone installed at home, and she spent hours finding out who had entertained relatives and where they were from; who had a new baby and what its name was, also names of all relatives; what family was now out of quarantine for scarlet fever; and who had gone back East to Fargo, North Dakota, to visit whom.

There was a certain style of writing that readers liked and my mother deplored. She would mutter, "House guests! Where *would* they put 'em — in the barn?" She abhorred "An elegant luncheon was served, consisting of (every item named), and a good time was had by all."

But she could not, all alone, reform the approved style of small-town social notes, so most of the time she had to play the game or disappoint the subscribers who knew how things ought to be.

Mr. Tallman, who owned the paper, always wore a brown printer's apron and ink on his face. He wrote the crime news himself; some of it was pretty nasty in those violent times, but he could tell what to sweep under the rug. He probably wrote the obituaries, too.

An obit in those days was not simply a statement of vital statistics. It was more like a blast of angelic trumpets at the heavenly gates, heralding the arrival of a saintly soul, even if the deceased had beaten his wife, alienated his children and drowned because he was drunk.

At the least, the eulogy could say he was ever a staunch Republican or he was an unswerving Democrat. Who was to know if he split his ticket?

For her printed news, my mother was paid so much per column inch. She typed it painfully, hunt & peck system, then sent away for a fingering chart and learned to use the right fingers on the right keys. She made me learn that way, too. I could type before I took typing in high school.

Whatever honest work was available, my mother did. I grew up in offices. She couldn't teach in spite of five years' experience in country schools; the Whitefish schools required teachers with a couple of years in "normal" school.

In spite of tight money, there was always some to drop in the collection plate at church. And some for charity. It was a family tradition that no matter what our situation was, there were others who were worse off.

Everybody worked forty-eight hours a week. My mother celebrated legal holidays by staying home and making cookies, pretending she had all the time in the world.

There were always the chickens to look after, and either the garden to work or cord wood to get cut and piled for winter or snow to shovel. I was also involved in all these, naturally.

The only thing she complained about was not having time for church work. She was cut off from her peers, her natural social group, the Ladies Aid Society. We went to their suppers and bought their baked goods, but she

77

couldn't *belong,* and a working woman carried a kind of stigma.

But she coped. We even had an awfully good time.

A Kind of Parable

WHEN MY FATHER DIED, Whitefish was still too new to have its own cemetary, so he was buried in the Conrad Cemetery in Kalispell, the county seat, 15 miles away. We didn't have a car — few people did — so it was not possible to take flowers to his grave except under unusual circumstances.

I remember one sad pilgrimage, perhaps a year and a half later, that my mother was able to arrange because a man we knew was driving to Kalispell anyway. There were, I think, two ladies besides my mother. The man delivered us and our flowers at the cemetery and promised to pick us up at a certain point in town late in the afternoon.

In addition to the flowers — whatever the ladies could pick to take along — we had a box of sandwiches. There was not even any discussion of eating lunch in a restaurant. Whatever that cost, it was too much.

After the visit to the cemetery, our little group walked along streets strange to us, looking for a place to sit down and eat. If there was a park, we didn't find it. But the houses had shade trees, and someone in our party got up courage enough to knock on a door and ask whether we could eat our lunch in the shady yard.

The people who lived there were a very old couple, very kind, not only willing but tremulously anxious to have us stop a while. They brought out a pitcher of cool drinking water to refresh us and gave their sympathy when they learned the nature of our errand.

The kind old lady then brought something I have never forgotten: rhubarb sauce. She explained that they had plenty and to spare; they had a rhubarb bed in the back yard. We ate the rhubarb sauce gratefully. It was sharp and sour, without any sugar.

When the old couple was in the house, I asked my mother, "Why wasn't there any sugar in the rhubarb?" and she answered, "Because they can't afford it," and wiped her eyes.

While we waited for time to pass, before starting out to meet the man with the car, I leaned back against the trunk of a gnarled apple tree. One of the ladies in our party hissed a warning. I turned to see what was wrong — and saw that the tree trunk was covered with a moving mass of worms.

Those good, kind people no doubt badly needed the fruit from that tree, but they couldn't afford worm killer any more than they could afford sugar. I almost cried.

I have never forgotten, or wanted to forget, that doleful day or those good, kind old people who were eager to share with us what they had, which was next to nothing. They were glad to have us there, timid strangers who came to their door, asking permission to sit in the shade. Life was brutal to them, but they were happy to have something to give.

Sometimes now, when I encounter grasping people or whiners or those who think the world doesn't give them enough, I remember the taste of sour rhubarb sauce, the hideous crawling worms on the apple tree and that white-haired couple who could expect no future better than their present. I remember that day when we strangers who had so little accepted with gratitude the bounty of those who had still less.

Some Inside Dope
on City Hall

ONE OF THE JOYS OF MY CHILDHOOD in Whitefish was watching Uncle George blow up stumps. When my family got there, the big tree stumps that had once made wagon traffic hazardous right in the center of town — on Central Avenue and Second Street — had been blasted out. But plenty of them were still left where they weren't wanted, like in people's yards and where they wished to plant a vegetable garden. The town had literally been hacked out of the forest.

Uncle George took care of stumps as a sideline. George Tayler was half the police force and, being on duty only during a twelve-hour shift, naturally he had time for what is now called moonlighting. Any man who was able and willing to use explosives to get rid of stumps was a public benefactor. I don't know where he developed his expertise, but he took some pride in it.

81

An important part of his equipment was the rusty, twisted framework of an object known as a sanitary couch. When in working condition, this piece of furniture opened up into a fairly uncomfortable bed big enough for two. One glimpse of Uncle George, tall, broad-shouldered, mustached like a proper lawman, dragging the wreckage of this couch and carrying an axe, and small children came running from all directions, to watch with open-mouthed admiration. He put on the best show in town. He never hinted that we were a nuisance, but he never let us forget that we were observing a very dangerous project in which we could get hurt if we didn't mind what he said. We minded.

We watched with awe while he made holes under the offending stump and put the dynamite in. We stayed right where he ordered while he dragged a bunch of fresh-cut jackpines over and built them into a protective pile to cover the stump. (Meanwhile more youngsters were running to the scene, but he had eyes in the back of his head and an air of command; he kept us all back from center stage.) He walked around his handiwork, studied it, moved a couple of trees a little. Suspense built so that his small-fry audience almost forgot to breathe.

Then he arranged the rusted wreckage of the sanitary couch on the pile. We yearned forward but prepared to turn and run. When everything was just so, he glared at us and yelled, "Run!" and we ran away as fast as we could scamper. So we didn't see what he did to cause the explosion — we assumed he lit the fuse with a match. Then he ran, too.

The big bang was wonderful. The couch-burdened jackpines lifted but didn't scatter far because the rusted metal skeleton weighed them down. There was a magnificent blast of thunder, the stump jumped out of the ground just as it was supposed to do, and small pieces of it rained down for several seconds. When Uncle George gave the all-clear signal, we ran to squabble over the pieces, mementoes of a great occasion. They had a lovely smell of earth and rotted wood and dynamite.

Once he blasted out a great big stump right beside our dining room window without even cracking the glass. If there were any kids watching when Saint George slew the dragon, they didn't have a bit more fun that we had when Uncle George blew up a stump.

My generation grew up with considerable respect for lawmen. We were assured at home and at school that they were our protectors. I had closer personal relationships with city government than most kids, because after my father died my mother worked in the Whitefish City Hall. In my flightier moments, I claim to have grown up in the police station.

The original City Hall was a rattletrap frame building with a stable out back, built to shelter the official city horse, but the city no longer had a horse when my memories begin. When someone needed a horse, he could rent one at Mr. Little's livery stable. Probably a horse was needed less often by police than by W. K. Trippet, City Engineer and Water Commissioner, to inspect the system by which we got water from sources several miles away in the mountains north of town.

My mother was assistant to Mr. Trippet in his capacity as water commissioner, and she was also the elected City Treasurer. I don't remember where the police station was in that old building. The water office was a big room inadequately heated with a wood-burning stove. I walked over there from school for lunch, sandwiches and a can of soup heated on the stove.

A new brick City Hall was built in 1917. There, the police office was right across the hall from the water department, and the big books in which my mother entered the city's financial affairs were kept in a vault that opened from the police room. Once an unwary mouse got locked in the vault and died there. In spite of frantic searching by Whitefish's Finest, the corpse was never found. You wouldn't believe that so small a body could smell so bad for so long.

My mother often had to work evenings on the city books in the police station. I usually went along to do my homework, run the adding machine and help check the tapes when totals didn't balance.

The night policeman (no longer Uncle George) was usually out when we were in. He was supposed to be out, because crimes seldom came to his office to be committed, and the local telephone girl could usually track him down. If he brought a drunk to the city jail in the basement, he hustled the offender past the open door in a hurry to spare us ladies a view of the seamier side of life. I found these occasional hassles much more interesting than running the adding machine or doing arithmetic.

There was an uncomfortable period in city politics when the night policeman was a surly fellow who didn't like having us there. He didn't care for patrolling the streets, preferring a leisurely game of solitare at his desk, and he must not even have had any friends in the back rooms of pool halls, where the fearless enforcers of the law often took refuge on cold winter nights. He did what he could to make life miserable for the City Treasurer. He brought in a tub of mash, confiscated from a moonshiner, and stored it in his office. The ingredients looked like wet bran and bloated prunes, and they smelled awful.

He wouldn't move that tub to some other place, either, like the jail or the fire hall; he maintained it was evidence being held for the trial of a moonshiner and he had to keep it under his direct control. So there it sat, with an occasional bubble rising to say "glub," to the great distress of my mother. She was an ardent prohibitionist and felt soiled by its mere presence. That tub of working mash never did smell as bad as the unfindable mouse; her objection was a matter of moral principle. But she lost the battle.

As often happens to people who work for government at any level, a day came when a candidate flourishing a new broom was elected Mayor. A friend of my mother's came hotfooting to tell her sadly, "He says he's going to fire you from both your city jobs."

"Let's see him try to fire the elected City Treasurer!" she said grimly. "He'll find he can't do it." And if he did try, he did indeed find out.

But the job in the Water Department was appointive. She gave the matter about three minutes of thought. Then she wrote out her resignation from that and handed it to me to deliver. (I must have inherited her ability to decide important matters fast. It may take me half a day to pick out a dress pattern, but on two occasions I have bought a house after considering it for an hour or so.)

Jobs for women were very scarce indeed. Before buckling down to looking for one, my mother decided we needed a short camping trip so she could get her wits together. Our blankets were strapped on our backpacks and we were lacing our boots when the manager of the local power company office appeared at the door.

"Our cashier is on vacation," he said apologetically,

"and everything is piling up and nobody can find anything, so could you maybe come down and help out for a few days until he gets back?"

She guessed she could, if he would wait till she changed clothes. The cashier never did get back, so she worked there temporarily for ten years until she resigned, remarried, and moved to Wisconsin. For most of that time she was also City Treasurer.

I worked in the city hall a couple of times myself some years later, but not for long. Once was as stenographer for the City Clerk and Attorney, starting at $20 a month with a promise of a $5 raise each month up to $50, which was supposed to satisfy my wildest dreams of avarice. There wasn't much to do — I wrote such nice minutes of one council meeting from my shorthand notes that my boss decided I should attend *all* the council meetings. When I asked for overtime pay on account of that night work (which was really horrid, a continuing series of fights), he fired me.

The next time, a Mayor asked if I'd like to work for the Water Commissioner because his girl had suddenly quit. I felt right at home in that office, but the current Water Commissioner — a friendly man until then — wouldn't talk to me. When I asked for orders, he grunted that he didn't care what I did. Before noon I ran out of things to do and asked him timidly what was wrong.

"I'm shocked that you're here!" he said bitterly. "You must know what happened!" I didn't, so he explained furiously: The Mayor had made passes at my predecessor, even chased her around her furnished room the night before, and when she fought in defense of her virtue, he fired her. (I hadn't guessed he was such a swinger.) I figured that we girls ought to stick together, so I told the

86

embattled Water Commissioner I was going to lunch and wouldn't be back. He smiled for the first time that day.

Come to think of it, the City of Whitefish probably still owes me half a day's pay, but I never had to run any footraces with the Mayor.

After those experiences with government in little old Whitefish, I never had the slightest interest in trying to get a job in Washington D.C. There's no telling *what* a girl might run into there.

The Preacher Kept a Cow

WHITEFISH WAS PRETTY RURAL when I was growing up. The Methodist minister kept a cow in a shed behind the parsonage next to the church, and supplied milk to some of his neighbors as well as for his own household. He wasn't vowed to poverty; it just happened to work out that way.

Most of the settled people in town raised their own vegetables. A garden was, in fact, a symbol of stability. Boomers and drifters didn't stay long enough to raise a garden. We had a big garden, and at a tender age I peddled the produce door-to-door from a market basket after some coaching from my mother. She said my approach — "You don't want to buy any nithe ripe peath, do you?" — wasn't quite ideal. It was negative, for one thing, and anyway people didn't want ripe peas, they wanted green ones.

We also raised chickens for additional income. My

mother was so fond of our first little flock of Rhode Island Reds that she named each hen, but she found it terribly upsetting to chop the head off a bird with a name, so she kept their descendants anonymous and impersonal.

While very young, I learned to talk chicken language, and I can still do it, but I never know what I'm saying. I can keep a hen's interest for a minute or so (they have a very short attention span) by clucking and making soothing chicken noises while she stares at me with one eye. Then she utters a horrified squawk and runs off to tell the other girls. Either she can't stand my accent or, in my ignorance, I have touched on some shocking subject that respectable hens simply do not discuss.

In looking after our flock under the tutelage of my mother I learned more about chickens than I ever wanted to know. We kept baby chicks with their mother hens in low pens covered with small-mesh wire so they couldn't get out and wandering cats couldn't get in, but the chicks *wanted* to be eaten. Normally I like cats better than chickens, but family loyalty makes a difference. In cases of our chickens vs. someone else's cat, I defended the chickens. A smart cat will prowl along a pen, lashing its tail and stirring up a ruckus until the chicks in their hysteria force their way out of safe refuge and right into kitty's jaws.

In the spring, I maintained a constant cat alert; my bedroom window looked down at the chickens. The yowls of the intruding cat and the shrieks of the hen would wake me. I'd grab my .22 calibre rifle and fire at the cat.

Once I hit one, but not fatally. Some little girls who lived a couple of blocks away told me with pride that they had found a poor hurt kitty in their shed, so they took care of it until it got well — to come back and eat more of our baby chicks.

There was always something to be done for those blasted fowls. In all seasons they had to be fed and watered. In winter, the bucket I lugged to the chicken house had warm water in it. On cold nights, I plodded through the snow to let down a burlap curtain across the front of the henhouse and hang up a lighted lantern; not that they wanted to read in bed, but that small heat kept their feet from freezing on the perches. In summer they had to be let out for an occasional treat of foraging for green food and bugs and then herded back to their run. Did you ever try to herd a hen? She won't go your way even if it's the way she wanted to go in the first place.

In spring, I dealt with hysterical setting hens that were so devoted that they wouldn't leave their nests for a lunch unless removed forcibly. I was midwife for hatching chicks that were struggling to get out of their shells but couldn't quite make it alone. This is tricky business. You can't help them too much or too soon or they'll die on you.

I have one happy memory of our flock. That is the pleasure of watching a hen take a dust bath in the rhubarb patch. She shuffles her chest in the dry dust and works it into her feathers. She languidly stretches one leg and one wing, then the other leg and wing. She digs with her beak at her itchy places. She clucks her satisfaction. Then she shuffles some more. Finally she shakes herself all over — the equivalent of mopping off with a nice big Turkish towel.

This performance combines, for the hen, two of humanity's pleasures that used to be rather rare: stretching out in a bathtub of good hot water and sitting on the front porch in the evening after the dishes were done and the bread set to rise and the wash put to soak.

The dust-bathing hen has no responsibilities. She has

raised her brood of chicks and parted from them without sadness. She has scratched around industriously and filled up with food. Now she can attend to her itchy places, and there is all that lovely fine dust in the pleasant shade of the rhubarb leaves. So with a clear conscience she relaxes and looks after her personal comfort, and you can't help wishing you were a hen.

For the benefit of a generation that never sees chickens on the hoof, let me explain that they do not occur in nature on a plate, cooked, or all naked and white on a little paper tray covered with plastic in a supermarket. In the adult stage they are covered with feathers, the color depending on the breed. To get a chicken to the consumer, somebody has to kill it, take the feathers off and remove the innards. All these steps are unpleasant. At our house, my mother performed the assassination and I did the rest and still had the best part of the job. She didn't *like* cutting a hen's head off with an axe, but she spoiled me.

We had very superior chickens, rose-comb Rhode Island Reds, so there was a fairly brisk market for setting eggs to be hatched and reared by other people's more plebeian hens. A setting of fifteen nice brown eggs sold for $1.50, a substantial sum. I don't know where my mother learned all she knew about chickens, but she sorted setting eggs carefully; they had no ridges and were all perfectly shaped.

One frugal purchaser bought some of our ordinary, cheaper eating eggs, hatched them and unwisely boasted about how cleverly she had fooled Mrs. Johnson. When she tried it the next year, not a single egg hatched, and she was pretty mad. Mrs. Johnson had divided the flock, and only the best hens were in with a rooster. Those whose eggs sold cheaper, for eating, were in the equivalent of a nunnery. Hens lay even if there's no rooster around, but their eggs are infertile.

Dear me, I have learned a lot of things that are of no value to me now — like cube root and the boundaries of nations that haven't existed since 1918.

It was my good fortune as a child to spend some happy times on the Millers' farm near Whitefish, the kind of farm that I think does not exist any more, at least not in the West. Changes in farming practices and sanitary laws have obliterated such small family farms.

What the Millers used to do, necessary in their time, is now illegal. They kept a herd of Holstein cows, cooled and bottled the milk in a shining-clean room off the kitchen, and delivered it in town from door to door every morning in time for breakfast. Nowadays the deck is stacked in favor of corporations with names like Dairiland or Medogold. Such spelling is supposed to make the product taste better.

The Millers came from the Midwest, Minnesota I think, and my folks, who came from Iowa, made their acquaintance at church. Their farm supported from five to seven adult human beings, four or five horses, the herd of Holsteins, a flock of busy chickens, several hives of bees, and a few pigs. The people, the animals and the land all contributed to the support of one another. That farm was a living entity, working and productive.

Mable Engelter guided me to the old Miller place in the summer of 1974. I couldn't have found it, because the road has been moved. The farm used to be a mile and half from town, a far piece on foot, not so far in a buggy behind a sorrel horse named Major. It's no distance at all by car if you can find it.

This is what it used to be like. Out front was a big

hayfield, where men and horses labored and sweated in the summer sun. There were a two-story white house, an unpainted horse barn with hay in the loft, a big new cow barn painted red, a tall silo, a bunkhouse, and various sheds. Back off all that were more fields, and then the dark woods began, swampy woods drained by ditches and harboring dangers that were not imaginary. They were called sink holes.

But before we get to the woods, let's pause in the farmyard, where there was always something going on — seldom dramatic, just interesting, Maybe one of the men harnessing a team of horses, or some cute black and white calves to pet in the corral, or a cat going about its lawful business, which was catching mice in the barns, or a hen emerging from a doorway with triumphant cackles, or the cows plodding out to pasture. Or one of the women coming out to scatter grain for the chickens, and the rooster, discovering it, taking all the credit and yelling to his harem, "Come on, girls, see what I've got for you! You can always depend on wonderful me!"

Once there was a colt named Dolly. Yes, yes, technically she was a filly, but everyone called her a colt. Dolly started out as a beautiful brown but turned gray while still a girl. Dolly scared me into shrieks once. When I wandered out eating bread-and-butter-and-sugar she fought me for it, and she was bigger than I was. She backed me into a corner, grabbed my snack and chewed a button off my sweater while getting the sugar that had spilled. I hadn't had enough experience with horses to understand that they're mad about sugar. I shrieked because I thought Dolly was going to eat *me*.

The farmyard was a fine place where something was always happening. Beyond the back hayfield was the forest, where dreadful things could happen because of the swamp. I remember only one that actually did, and that probably wasn't back of the Miller place, but it was somewhere in those dark woods. A small boy wandered off and, in spite of massive searches by many volunteers, no sign of him was ever found.

Probably he fell into a sinkhole. These were of variable sizes, some only a few feet across, filled with standing water, and not easy to see. Somebody went to the trouble of marking one of them by putting a tall, dead lodgepole pine down into it. The top few feet of the lodgepole stuck up above the surface of the water, so sinkholes were not, as local legend said, bottomless, but they were near enough to it to be fatal. It wasn't wise to go plunging around in those wet woods in any hurry. One walked with care.

The Millers had a cabin out there, occasionally inhabited by a solitary woodcutter who was paid by the cord for the firewood he cut and stacked. A corduroy road led to the cabin. Corduroy roads were a frontier invention that could be built through swampy forest with the materials that grew there — trees — plus an axe and a lot of muscle and some big nails if available. Such a road is built by laying small logs close together across wooden stringers. It moves up and down in the muck under the gingerly placed hooves of horses, and a person walking gets his feet wet, but at least the walker doesn't sink up to his knees, and a wagon can make progress without getting totally bogged down.

The woods were fascinating. Skunk cabbage grew there, with great gaudy yellow flowers, and pale blue clematis almost the color of air, and pink lady slippers and mint. Sometimes ghostly white Indian pipes heaved up right through dry spots in the road. Often I heard grouse drumming, sounding like someone trying to start a small gasoline engine.

The Millers' cows were milked twice a day — by hand. When I visited the farm I never got up early enough to supervise the morning milking and was not awfully welcome at the barn in the evening, either. The reason given was that I might get in the men's way. Mostly, I think, it was because I shouldn't hear the language they sometimes used to the cows. Some cows like to switch a tail in the milker's face; some try hard to put a foot in the bucket or, better yet, kick it over when it's three-quarters full. So a milker has a right, even a duty, to reprove them without being hampered by the presence of a little girl.

Once I wanted to learn to milk. The lesson lasted about three minutes. The teacher announced, "Your hands are too small and at the rate you're going you'll dry up the cow." Later my mother remarked, "The smartest thing a woman can do is *not* learn to milk. If you can, you'll have to." She had carefully never learned.

In the fall of 1918 came the great epidemic of Spanish influenza. Sick people took care of sicker people. Many of them died. Public gatherings were forbidden. The three doctors never got any sleep. When school closed for an indefinite time, my mother sent me out to stay with the Millers. She went on working, as everyone did who still could. So I was there on the day when the great news came: The war is over! She heard it in town and telephoned it to the farm.

Grandma Miller stopped dead in her tracks: now her youngest son wouldn't have to go. He was in a student training group at the University. She pulled herself together and smiled at me and said, "You can tell the bees."

I was puzzled. "What should I tell them?" I often talked to horses and chickens and calves, but bees never seemed very friendly. Besides, they were all put to bed for the winter in their hives out by the garden.

"Just tell them the war is over," she said. So I put on my sweater and went outside to the row of beehives. This custom I had never heard of before and have heard of only once since. It is very old; there is an obligation to tell the bees about important events. Otherwise they won't thrive.

I was then, and still am, timid about undertaking for the first time something I don't know how to do. What was the right way to tell the bees? There was no way to find out, so I simply did it, hoping there was no wrong way. The silent hives were bundled up for winter. I walked along the row of them and spoke politely to each hive, repeating, "The war is over," having to take it for granted that some of them were listening. "The war is over," I told them all. Then I went back into the warm house, my peculiar duty done.

That night or the next one there was a big celebration in town, and everybody went who wasn't sick in bed with the flu. But more vividly than the glee of the celebration and the patriotic music of the Whitefish Boys Band I remember those few minutes when I walked along by the silent hives on the 11th day of November, 1918, telling the bees. It was a strange and memorable privilege. And it was the only time in my life that I ever spoke gently to bees. My normal reaction when I see one coming is to shriek and run for cover.

In this age of specialization, lots of ranch kids don't know any more about milk than city kids do, because Daddy raises grain or sheep or hay or beef cattle. Milk comes in waxed cartons at a supermarket, as skim milk, low fat,

95

homogenized, half-and-half, heavy cream, buttermilk and chocolate flavor. For these kids I must explain that it doesn't come that way naturally. It comes in cows. At least cow's milk does.

A cow has four spigots, but just plain whole milk comes from all of them. Her calf can't have a treat of strawberry malt, no matter how much he whines and teases. If you leave this plain milk alone in a pan, nice yellow cream will rise to the top. Ladle it off, let it sour, churn it, and you get butter. What's left is buttermilk. Or you can put the fresh whole milk through a machine called a separator; cream comes out a little pipe and skim milk comes out a bigger one.

No cream rises on the milk I buy, because it's homogenized — forcibly stirred up. And it never sours; it just spoils. This is progress, I suppose. If the Millers had homogenized their milk, they would have lost all their customers, because people used that risen cream in coffee. The milk was delivered in shining clean glass bottles every single morning. Mine comes in disposable cartons on Monday and Thursday, except when Monday falls on a holiday. I've never laid eyes on the man who leaves it in a box at the front door.

The Millers' milk was delivered by a quick-moving young cousin of Grandma Miller, Ruth Day. Everybody in town knew and admired her. No blizzard stopped her. She rode in an open buggy pulled by a sorrel horse named Major, with the milk bottles in the back of the rig. The lithe way she leaped out, grabbed the right number of bottles, ran up to the right houses with them, picked up the empty bottles, and leaped back into the buggy was a sight to behold — preferably from inside a nice warm house.

Sometimes I spent a weekend at the farm and rode back

home with her on Monday morning, so I know how bleak and dark and bitter cold those winter mornings were, how deep the snow could be before the city's horse-drawn snowplow came through and how slippery was the ice on the buggy step.

One summer when I was about halfway through college, my mother spent a week of vacation at the Millers' cabin in the woods. By that time they had sold out to Joe Moneghan, who had a milk route in town. I worked at her office that week — she was cashier at the Mountain States Power Company — and commuted from the cabin.

This involved getting up at 5 A.M. for a quick breakfast, which she cooked on an old wood stove. For me there was a hike through the woods on the corduroy road to the farm, a ride into town on the milk wagon, a change from hiking clothes to a dress at home, and another walk to the office. Returning to the cabin after work (after changing clothes again) there was no ride even part of the way. We ate supper by kerosene lamplight and then went to bed. There was nothing else to do and no time to do it anyway.

My mother had a fine time with the creatures of the wild in the daytime. She scared the wits out of a porcupine, which stayed under the porch floor most of the time while she poked rags down to catch its quills. She completely upset the life style of a buck deer that was accustomed to drinking from a pool near the cabin. The pool bred mosquitos, so she put some kerosene on it. When the buck innocently dipped his thirsty muzzle through that film of kerosene, he just about had a fit. She was still laughing when I got there hours later. The resident wild life was mightily relieved when we moved back to town.

The Millers' two-story white house was the heart of the entity that was the farm. Downstairs there were four rooms

— the kitchen, the dairy room (sacred to milk and the cream separator and a big ice box and used for nothing else), the dining room (which became the living room when the supper dishes were cleared away, because there was a fancy big lamp that hissed and gave good light for reading), and a small sitting room with a slippery sofa and an upright piano. The Millers' youngest son, Lyle, played the piano very well. Upstairs were two dormitory-type bedrooms.

Ah, the kitchen! There was a big wood-burning range whence came marvelous food (Grandma Miller was a fabulous cook) and even the convenience of a small hand pump at one end of the sink so nobody had to carry in water. Somebody did, however, have to carry out the swill pail quite often. That little pump was a fine thing to have, but you had to be careful never to leave the handle up or it would lose its ability to bring up water. Then one of the men would have to prime it, with suitable grumbling because the men had better things to do.

When Mable took me out to see the old Miller place, decades later, it was a farm no more, but just a place to live in the country. The field where men and horses had toiled under the summer sun to raise hay and grain produced a mammoth crop of useless golden dandelions, like other places nearby that had once been farms. The fields were too small to work with modern machinery, and who remembers how to harness or drive a team? The buildings were gone as if they had never been, even the tall silo and the big red cowbarn. The white house was gone, replaced by a low modern one where two small children played in the yard.

The pleasant young woman we talked to there had never heard of the Millers or the Moneghans, who bought the farm from them. She named half a dozen people who had owned it in recent years; I had never heard of any of them. She and her husband, a doctor in town, and their two little boys were renters.

The menacing black forest at the back was a frail green; it has been cleared off and thin new growth has replaced it. I didn't have the heart to ask whether the sinkholes are still there. It's better to remember the dark mysteries of that swamp as they used to be. The living farm was long dead and long forgotten.

Those utterly useless fields of dandelions were like a knife in my heart. Ghosts of sweating men and horses and the crops they raised were there; that was no place for the rich earth to be idle and grown to weeds!

A year later I went back and found a change and felt a whole lot better. Roy Duff owned the old place — a busy man, a take-charge man; he operated several businesses. Just catching him took half the afternoon. He drove me out to the farm.

He was getting some good out of the place. His son lived in the cozy new house. By the road Roy had put up four big quonsets to house his nineteen buses. Quonsets aren't pretty, but they didn't offend me like those useless dandelions. The old small fields were merged with other small and useless fields, planted to grain.

The fences are down, big machines can work and the earth lives again and is green with crops.

In Whitefish some people still have vegetable gardens, but not so big as ours was. Fresh produce is shipped in from California, even in winter.

Where our big garden was, and the chicken house and all that, there's a new house inhabited by people I don't know. The Methodist preacher doesn't keep a cow. You

can't hear a rooster herald the dawn anywhere in town.
Such rusticity is probably forbidden by city ordinance,
along with outdoor privies.

Confessions of
A Telephone Girl

I USED TO BE A SWITCHBOARD OPERATOR in
Whitefish. Not everybody had a telephone — at $1.75 a
month on a four-party line, it was a luxury that lots of
people could do without.

I was relief operator at Whitefish for two years in high
school and every summer when I was home from the
University. I started at age fourteen, and it's a good thing
there were no laws effectively restricting child labor, because I needed that money to help pay for an education.

The Mountain States Power Company had both the
electric power and telephone franchises in our neck of the
woods. The local manager was a portly, pompous man
named A. P. Tills. The telephone girls carried on a running
battle with him, which nobody won.

The roster of operators included three girls "on steady,"
each working eight hours a day with one day off every two
weeks; one girl "on relief," who worked those off shifts
(every Sunday and every other Friday night); and one

who was learning. She came in whenever she felt like it, helped out or got in the way for a few hours, and didn't get paid at all.

A girl on steady, working 56 hours one week and 48 the next, got $50 a month. The relief girl was paid $1.65 for eight hours. If she worked part of a shift for one of the steady girls, that girl paid her 20 cents an hour. When I was relieving, I maintained that $1.65 divided by eight hours ought to be 21 cents, but the steady girls stood shoulder to shoulder against inflation.

These jobs were much in demand. There were usually two or three girls hopefully waiting for a chance to learn. The relief operator (unless she was me, not intending to make a career of it) hoped that one of the steady girls would get married, move away, or drop dead.

We all taught the learners willingly; it gave us status to have someone to admonish, because nobody hesitated to admonish us. And any of us could tell, after a couple of hours, whether she was ever going to be any good. If she was phlegmatic and didn't get upset when she made a mistake, there wasn't much hope. Slow and steady did not win that race. The plowhorse type would never learn to be nimble, to keep track of the time on a long distance call while handling a lot of local calls and trying to hunt down a doctor and the Great Northern call boy. The fire-horse type worked out best — nervous, dedicated, quick, To this day, when the timer on my electric range buzzes, I jump a foot.

There were no flashing lights on our switchboard. It had rows of black eyes, each with a number under it. When a subscriber wanted to make a call, he ground a crank. The little black eye above his number flipped over and showed red. Our board was modern enough, though, so that the operator didn't grind a crank to ring. She pulled a little peg called a key — and it had better be the right key or she'd ring somebody a blast in the ear, which was a dreadful thing to do because it hurt.

The board was a vast expanse of eyes, with, at the base, a dozen or so pairs of plugs on cords for connecting and an equal number of keys for talking, listening, and ringing. On a busy day these cords were woven across the board in a constantly changing, confusing pattern; half the people using telephones were convinced that Central was incompetent or hated them, and Central — flipping plugs into holes, ringing numbers, trying to remember whether 44 wanted 170K or 170L, because if she went back and asked him, he'd be sure she was stupid — was close to hysterics.

It was every operator's dream that when her ship came in she would open all the keys on a busy board, yell "To hell with you," pull all the plugs and march out in triumph, leaving everything in total chaos. Nobody ever did. We felt an awful responsibility toward our little corner of the world. We really helped keep it running, one girl at a time all by herself at the board.

We were expected to remember quite a lot of things. There were two rural lines with lots of people on them and multiple rings, like three shorts and one long for a store out in the woods somewhere. Mostly these subscribers tended to their own affairs and did their own handle grinding, calling between isolated lumber camps, timber claims, and ranger stations. We were supposed to ignore them unless they buzzed one long ring. That meant they wanted the switchboard to connect them with someone on another line. The theory was fine. It just didn't work very well.

Consider: A girl is trained to stab a plug into every hole

102

that buzzes, but she is also trained to ignore two of them. That's hard enough. But she is supposed to NOT ignore them if one long buzz sounds. When there are buzzes all over the board, she probably does the wrong thing. Either she forgets to ignore those two lines, says "Number, please?" and is told by an impatient caller twenty miles away to get off the line, or she remembers to ignore them and doesn't notice when one of them gives a long buzz that she's supposed to answer.

So way out there on a mountain somewhere a frustrated smoke chaser grinds the crank harder and harder and gets madder and madder because he has a forest fire to report and why the hell doesn't Whitefish answer? When she finally remembers not to ignore that long buzz, the smoke chaser naturally gives her a piece of his mind, hot off the griddle, and her feelings are hurt and maybe she cries. It's a wonder ALL the forests didn't burn up, with the flames fanned by gusts of high emotion.

We were also supposed to keep in mind that two other lines were pay stations, and when anyone phoned from there, it cost money. We were suspicious of anyone who was willing to pay a nickel for a local call. He was obviously up to no good. Why didn't he call from the pool hall? So he wanted privacy, did he? He didn't get it. A charming fellow I had met while swimming over at Whitefish Lake once called from a pay phone. Recognizing his voice, of course I kept the key open. He made an appointment with a fallen woman over at the Red Flats, so after that I didn't need any more swimming instruction from him.

On a pay-station call, when the operator got the called number to answer, she said, "Hold the line, please," closed the key, opened the key to the pay phone, said, "I have your number. Deposit five cents, please," and waited until the nickel clanked. Then she connected both lines and advised benignly, "Go ahead."

For long distance it was harder, counting clanks of varying tones for various coins and doing mental arithmetic. Mr. Tills collected the money from the pay stations once a month. There was always too much money, and this he couldn't forgive. We always thought he ought to be pleased. But we were supposed to make out a ticket for every dratted five-cent call, and when we were busy, we couldn't. When the monthly day of accounting came, we quivered under the lash of his tongue — "Two dollars and sixty-five cents too much in zero — what do you girls think you're *doing*?" We would gladly have divided the surplus among ourselves to keep him happy, but he had the key to the money boxes.

On one ghastly occasion the total was almost nine dollars short, and of course collecting too little money was worse than collecting too much. It was my fault, too. A man had phoned all the way to New York from the pay station at the Cadillac Hotel. New York, mind you! Who ever heard of such a thing?

The combined efforts of operators in cities all across the United States, their voices getting fainter with distance as they bandied around a lot of bewildering code abbreviations, put the call through in a hurry. It didn't take more than a couple of hours. And I was so flushed with triumph when the connection was completed that I forgot to tell him to drop in his money. By the time the shortage was discovered, he had left town — the rat — and the hotel had no forwarding address for him. Mr. Tills came close to apoplexy.

There were two other lines about which we had to remember something special: "Don't say 'Number, please.' Say 'Whitefish.' " Those lines were long distance connecting Kalispell, and we stood, in relation to any Kalispell operator, as an erring child to a stern stepmother who is a practicing witch. All our long-distance calls went or came through Kalispell. Why, over there they had an operator who handled nothing but long distance!

We couldn't really imagine so idyllic a situation. A girl at our switchboard was everything — local, long distance, and information. We also turned on the fire alarm and the police signal. We used to tell inquirers what time it was until somebody missed a train because our clock was slow. After that, Mr. Tills made us refer such inquiries to the Great Northern depot, and the agent on duty there didn't like it a bit. Some subscribers even expected us to know whether No. 2 was going to be on time, but the railroad didn't think we ought to be responsible for information like that.

For Mr. Tills, life was a constant battle, him against us. We seldom came up to his standard. He had spent some years in Chicago, and he mentioned it often. Telephone users in Whitefish didn't come up to his standard, either. Everybody tended to be too informal.

If Mrs. Smith asked for 73 X, which was her sister, and we knew 73 X wouldn't answer because she wasn't home, we were likely to say, "She's at 190-L — I'll ring there." This was fine with Mrs. Smith and her sister, but Mr. Tills couldn't stand it. They didn't do things that way in Chicago. We were supposed to keep ringing 73-X until Mrs. Smith got tired and hung up or we got tired and announced, "That number does not answer."

Since our switchboard had no lights to flash on or off, the only way a girl could find out when people had finished a conversation was to open the key, listen, and inquire,

105

"Are you waiting? Are you through?" If nobody said anything, she pulled the plugs. If somebody did say something, it was usually, "No, we're not through. Get off the line!"

The telephoning public had a dark suspicion that we spent our spare time listening in, and very often the public was right. Mr. Tills felt that listening in was a crime just short of manslaughter. They didn't do it in Chicago. Of course not. Nobody in Chicago knew anybody.

Another thing they didn't do in Chicago was to ring a number that the calling party couldn't look up because she had mislaid her glasses or the baby had torn that page out of the phone book. In cases like this, Mr. Tills expected us to assume another aspect of our triple personality. The local operator became Information. When requested to ring Charlie Turner's house, she mustn't admit that she knew the number. She was supposed to refer the calling party to Information. Then she said, "This is Information. May I help you?" and after letting enough time elapse to look up "Turner, Charles," which she didn't need to do, she announced his number.

Naturally the calling party then said, "All right, ring it, will you?" But Information was too superior to ring numbers; all *she* did was reveal them. So Information said with a tinge of reproach, "I will connect you with the operator." Thereupon she clicked the key a couple of times to indicate that big doings were afoot and came back on the line to say, "Number, please?"

This nonsense puzzled the customers, who knew very well that there was only one girl on the board, so what was all the fuss about? But Mr. Tills liked the formality: it was as close as possible to the way they did it in Chicago.

Sometimes in the evening when he had nothing better

106

to do, he strolled around downtown and checked up on us from various phones. He was seldom successful in catching an operator doing something wrong. We recognized his voice. We recognized a lot of voices. Voices were our business. If he tried to make a girl mad by being grumpy or downright rude, she became sweeter and sweeter; she dripped the honey of courtesy until he was up to his ankles in it.

If he tried to catch her knowing a number without referring to her all-wise other self, Information, she gave him more key clicks than anyone else got; also she kept him waiting a while and came back on the line to apologize abjectly for the delay and explain that the board was terribly busy. This was part of our continuing war with Mr. Tills. We insisted that only a genius with four hands could handle the job. He was convinced that we had nothing to do and really should mop the floor once in a while.

Once he tried to prove we weren't overworked and couldn't possibly need two girls during the busiest part of the day. (Occasionally a day operator, pushed past the endurance point, simply burst into hysterical tears.) He would have us keep an accurate count of local calls. So he gave us a little gadget that we were supposed to tap every time we plugged in. If there was anything an overworked operator didn't need, it was one more gadget to keep track of. Naturally, what we did was ignore it until a lull came; then we caught up with our tapping, plus a good big bonus on account of resentment.

One of the perquisites of Mr. Tills' job as manager was a rent-free apartment just down the hall from the room the switchboard was in, and one of his duties (he said) was to supervise; i.e., to snoop and try to catch the night operator taking a nap. He removed the lock from our door, leaving

107

a big round hole suitable for peering through. We always knew when he was there, because the floor squeaked. Mr. Tills had an affliction that made one of his eyes roll around sometimes. It was enough to stand your hair on end to glance over at the peep hole and see that whirling eye.

One night a newly trained girl on her first all-alone shift saw it and was terrified — but not paralyzed. With great presence of mind, she switched on the downtown light that signaled the police, rang the police station and left the key open so the night cop could hear her death struggle if it came to that, and then ran to the open window and screamed for help. It was all terribly embarrassing for Mr. Tills. After that there was a big cork in the peep hole.

I came home from the University one June to find that a new girl had been hired, and she was trying to reform our methods, also Mr. Tills'. She worked in Minneapolis, which was almost as awesome as Chicago, both being big cities way back east. She was determined to introduce big-city usages in little old Whitefish. For her, the Great Northern depot was nigh-un nigh-un and Hori's Cafe was thu-rrree thu-rrree. She said "Oppiteh" when she meant operator, and her "Number please" came out like "No place." These elegancies confused the customers quite a lot, they being used to our home-grown pronunciation. Unless, I suppose, they had lived in Minneapolis.

We resented her, partly because she was married and didn't need the job, but we grudgingly admired her, too, because she bullied Mr. Tills and sometimes seemed to have him on the ropes. After all, his gospel about how they did things in Chicago was only hearsay; he had never been an oppiteh there. But Florence, or whatever her name was, had the True Word about Minneapolis from personal experience.

She yearned to be our Chief Oppiteh and sometimes claimed she was, but Mr. Tills said she wasn't. Our real Chief Oppiteh was in Kalispell. We never laid eyes on her. We thought of her as a goblin that would get us if we didn't watch out, but we loved her as compared with Florence. So we went along as before, without any resident Chief Oppiteh. In Whitefish we were all first among equals.

When Florence departed, she left us a legacy. She used very fancy penmanship on long distance tickets, and for a while we all put little circles over our i's instead of dots.

I was a pretty good operator but not the best one Whitefish ever had. We had two girls in the years I worked there who were wonders. Carrie and Faye were the fastest draws in the West. Either of them could ring a number (front key plus a button for L, K, Y or X) with the left hand while flipping a back plug into a hole with the right hand and caroling "That party doesn't answer" with no hands to somebody else. Meanwhile she could remember that 90 had blinked before 144 and therefore deserved to be answered first and, when she had a second to spare, open two or three keys to inquire "Are you waiting? Are you through?" and pull out the plugs without disconnecting anybody. Those girls' hands darted around like a pair of hummingbirds.

Along with all this, Faye or Carrie could remember that when Kalispell called back to report, "On your 15 to Spokane, W.H." the man who had placed the call on Ticket 15 at the Cadillac Hotel pay station wasn't in the booth any more but she should ring the desk clerk, who would trot down the hall to his room to get him.

W.H. meant "We have the party you want, anyway within shouting distance, so now try to find yours." W.H.L. meant "We have the party on the line with the key open, so let's be formal." H.L. meant "Hold the line, I'll be right back." D.A. stood for "Doesn't answer; might as well give up." N.A. was less final — "No answer, but remind me later and I'll try some more." A.Y. meant "The calling party will talk to anyone who answers at that number." A.B. meant he would settle for anybody who could talk business. B.Y. meant "The line is busy."

We never knew why long distance operators had to communicate in that esoteric way. We simply accepted the idea that ordinary people trying to connect with someone far away were not supposed to know what was going on until one or another operator emerged from the sacred mystery and translated into plain language. I loved those code letters. They made me feel like part of an international spy ring instead of a relief operator whose eight-hour shift was worth $1.65.

Automatic telephone equipment sometimes baffles me. If I get a wrong number, I have to accept the idea that I dialed it wrong. It was nicer in the old days, when the calling party knew darn well that Central had made the mistake and should, therefore, be chewed out. If I make a person-to-person call to Los Angeles and it isn't completed, the ticket — if there is one — gets lost in some orderly shuffle at the local switchboard and an hour later I have to give all that information over again. Sixty years ago, at the Whitefish switchboard, the girl would have been all agog to keep trying on that call as often as Kalispell would let her. But nobody ever called Los Angeles. We weren't even sure how to pronounce it.

We took care of a lot of little things that a dial system won't do for you. If a brakeman's wife, expecting the doctor to phone because the baby was sick, asked us to ring lightly because Henry had to catch some sleep before

110

going out on his run, we rang lightly.

Sometimes we were trapped. When the roundhouse whistle wailed over and over, we braced for a flood of calls because that signal called out the wrecker. Somewhere east or west a train was in bad trouble. Men might be hurt, might be dying. Frantic wives phoned, demanding the dispatcher's office, wanting to know at least in which direction that wrecked train was. But everybody who might know was busy getting a crew together, making arrangements for the emergency, and couldn't answer such calls. All we could do was help the women worry. A dial system can't even do that.

Another difference between now and then is that teen-agers didn't monopolize telephones. They hadn't thought of it. Most of them were half scared to use the telephone. In fact, teen-agers hadn't even been invented back the early 1920's. There were just big kids, little kids, and babies.

One of our sins that I'm not sure Mr. Tills ever caught onto was what we called "talkin' to a fellah." Late evenings and at night there was nothing much to do at the switchboard. When a girl had read all the dog-eared confession magazines, frowning because some other girl had already clipped the coupons that would bring a free sample of face powder, life was pretty dull. There wasn't room to lay out a game of solitaire. So when some man about town called in and crooned, "Hey, kid, you wanna talk?" she usually did.

The conversation was utterly pointless, small talk at its most pulverized. Neither party said anything worth listening to or answering. But the idea was romantic. This was a kind of pillow talk that involved no obligation. It was voice to voice, not face to face. Mostly Central murmured, "H-m-m? Umm, not really....Umm, maybe...Oh, you go

111

on!'' Followed by a gurgle of giggles.

A really bold romeo might ask for the privilege of walking Central home after her shift was over (the evening shift, that is; nobody cared to walk home the night girl who got off at seven in the morning), and she might lead him on a little. But she probably refused him in the end and sneaked out the back way, just in case he might be the type who wouldn't take No for an answer. She didn't really want to meet him. He might be an absolute monster. She just liked the sound of his voice, and he helped pass the time.

I carried on an affair intermittently all one summer with a smokechaser far away in the woods. Both of us had to stay awake. He could make a conversation about nothing last until 3:00 A.M. and sound like Don Juan arranging a seduction without ever saying a thing I couldn't have repeated to my mother. I remember his voice fondly and with gratitude. Murmuring and cooing, we kept each other awake while he guarded the forest and I took care of Whitefish.

Shorty Gammel, Funny-Man

I'VE NEVER KNOWN A MAN CALLED SHORTY who wasn't likeable. We had a Shorty in Whitefish. Almost everybody loved him — maybe because he seemed happy. Why wouldn't he seem happy? He was single and had his whole paycheck to spend as he saw fit.

Shorty was a lineman, usually the only lineman, for Mountain States Power Company, so everybody knew him. He connected up the electricity for new customers; he installed all the telephones; he took care of complaints about both electric and telephone service.

I knew him better than most people did, because my mother was for ten years cashier in the company office, and I often worked with her after school to help balance the day's business so we could go home for supper soon after closing time, which was five o'clock. When I worked as relief telephone operator, I came to know Shorty even better.

113

It took me a while to get over being afraid of him, because he spoke something that was his version of the English language, but sounded foreign until you got used to it. He wasn't foreign; he came, he said, from Fuhjinny. I've met lots of people from Virginia, but none of them ever sounded like Shorty Gammel. His first name was Vernon, but few people knew that.

Shorty wasn't unusually short. He was pudgy and very homely, with a big nose, green eyes and weather-reddened skin. Like any lineman, he jingled and clanked when he was on the job, because he had so many tools attached to him. A man who is about to climb a wooden pole that doesn't have metal spikes in it for steps wears heavy climbers strapped onto his legs; the climbers have spur-like projections for jabbing into the pole. He wears a heavy sling belt to hold him upright on the pole while he works. This is in addition to the belt that keeps his pants up. Shorty purely hated to climb poles, and I don't know how he happened to get into his line of work.

Shorty was a gregarious man — a born joiner. He belonged to about every club or fraternal organization for which he was eligible. He belonged to the Volunteer Fire Department and for a long time was fire chief. He took his responsibilities very seriously. Once he was upset enough about complaints from the other firemen to confide in me. Translated from his strange version of English, what he said boiled down to, "They're mad about the kind of fire drills I set up for 'em. They say I'm too tough, make 'em take the fire truck to places where there ain't no handy hydrants. That's exactly my idea. I don't take 'em where the hydrants *is* — I take 'em where they *ain't!*"

Since fire strikes indiscriminately, without regard to the presence of handy hydrants for the big hose, this idea of

114

having drills where hydrants ain't seems eminently sensible. Our firemen learned to improvise.

One thing Shorty didn't belong to was any church, but he devotedly attended every fund-raising supper that the ladies put on, no matter what their denomination. He usually brought along a couple of other working men — all of them well scrubbed and well combed and wearing clean work clothes. Shorty paid a little more than the announced price. The ladies made much of him and called him Mr. Gammel. He always acted embarrassed at these affairs, but church ladies were notably good cooks and he was a bachelor who ate in restaurants.

If any of these same ladies had invited him to her home for a family meal, he would probably have jumped on the next train and left Whitefish forever. There was, between a middle-aged working-stiff bachelor and a respectable family, an unbridgeable gulf.

Shorty loved to talk, but conversaton was frustrating for him and everyone else involved because of his peculiar pronunciation. He talked too fast; he stuttered when excited; and he was excited about something most of the time. Words poured out, but meaning was often hard to come by. So everybody laughed, partly to cover embarrassment, and Shorty was known far and wide as a very funny fellow. He laughed like a happy baby, with his mouth wide open and most of his tongue showing.

He was so comical that you wouldn't have thought he had a care in the world. But he had plenty of them. Whatever he had done before coming to Whitefish, he hadn't gone to school very much. He could read, but he did it without pleasure. He had to read work orders, telling him where to hook up or disconnect electric service, where to install or remove telephones, where there was some

115

kind of trouble.

He probably couldn't spell, but his handwriting was so utterly awful that you really couldn't tell. He had to write something on work orders to show that he had done his duty, and sometimes I had to figure out what he scribbled and signed "V. Gammel." I couldn't read his notes, but learned how to guess what he meant. (I should have gone into cryptography.)

The part of his job he hated most was cutting off service when some family's light bill had gone unpaid for too long. I don't think he ever really did it. He accepted the work order and went out grumbling, returning after a while with the money. But it was seldom the right amount of money, as it would have been if he had collected it in nickels and dimes. No, he'd have a ten-dollar bill that had to be changed, proving (he never caught on to this) that he couldn't bear to leave some family with no lights, but was paying the bill himself.

After A. P. Tills came to be the company's local manager, he made Shorty's life hell. Jealousy, no doubt, because everybody loved Shorty, but who loved Mr. Tills? Tills humiliated him by claiming that Shorty was too old for his job, that he had lost his nerve for climbing poles. Well, Shorty was there before Tills came and he was still there after Tills left.

Tills liked to remind him in front of other people that he got free rent. (So did Tills, in an apartment on the second floor of the power company building.) Shorty did, indeed, get free rent — in a shack on the alley. When I was about fifteen, I had to go there with him once to get some of his clothes. We were both a little embarrassed about it, but I had my mother's permission.

I went to Shorty's shack to pick up my costume for the

116

high school play. I had the role of a society gentlemen with a French name. Come to think of it, the play took place in Paris and all the characters had French names. I played a male role because Whitefish High School was short of boys in those days and the girls had to do just about everything.

The play was, of course, a comedy. Even if it hadn't been intended that way, casting the short, chunky Johnson girl as a society gentleman would have made it funny.

Shorty Gammel had an outstanding wardrobe because he was a bachelor without dependants and a shining light in almost every local organization except the Ladies Aid. He grinned and said he would lend me his dress suit. I had never seen one before in real life. But there was a problem about a shirt to go with it. (Maybe his dress shirt was dirty.) So he hunted out his red wool shirt — the one he wore when the volunteer Fire department dressed up for parades.

I must have been a doll in that outfit — the bright red shirt with the cutaway black jacket and pants that had to have cuffs pinned up several inches. They were too big around the middle, too. The audience laughed when I came on stage. The people could tell right away that the play was *supposed* to be funny, so they relaxed and enjoyed it. No doubt Shorty bought a ticket and attended. He went to *every* public event that took place after working hours.

When I went to borrow his dress suit, I saw how he lived. This was no sybaritic pad for a swinging bachelor. His shack was bare and unpainted inside, with a minimum of furniture. That was standard for bachelors, but I was shocked by the glare of the electric light in broad daylight. It was almost blinding. He explained casually, "I never

117

turn it off. I sleep with the light on and if it goes out, that wakes me up — means there's a power failure.''

A power failure was a terrible thing in Shorty's life. It meant trouble, danger, possible disaster, and everybody in town would blame him for it. I still shudder at his dedication. Imagine being so used to sleeping in a glare that you wake up if the room goes dark! Shorty didn't even know he was a slave to his job. He thought he worked 48 hours a week like other people.

As a determined bachelor, Shorty kept one part of his active social life a dark secret. That part involved women. I hadn't even thought about this until Lulu got her hooks into him. Lulu wasn't her name, but it will do. She's dead now, but then she was young and rapacious, and she didn't follow Shorty's rule that his lady friends must keep out of sight. She showed up at the back door of the company's building one day and demanded to see him. He gave her some money and was grumpy for a couple of days. Lulu was about two years older than I and we had been in school together until she quit to devote more time to her chosen profession.

Shorty Gammel was good-natured and obliging, born to be imposed upon. Plenty of people took advantage of him. There was an elderly woman in Whitefish — call her Mrs. Smith — who often heard somebody moving around in her attic. I heard about Mrs. Smith's attic when I was relief telephone operator. She must have worn out her grown children and her neighbors with the oft-told tale; also the local police and probably her pastor. So who was left to protect her from the attic? Shorty, of course.

Every few days, especially in the evening, she phoned Central and announced, "I wish to speak to Mr. Gammel.'' All the operators adored Shorty, so we never could find him for her, even if he happened to be three feet away repairing a cord on the switchboard.

Since he was such a gadabout and his phone number was not listed, Mrs. Smith was willing to settle for Mr. Tills as second choice, and any of us was delighted to ring *him* for her. He stopped that with an edict: We must never, never ring him if the calling party was Mrs. Smith. So we had to tell her we couldn't reach Mr. Tills, either — he was out on important business.

Thus balked in her efforts to reach either Shorty or Mr. Tills, Mrs. Smith left a message: "Tell Mr. Gammel there is someone in my attic." Bang went the receiver. We told him, of course, laughing merrily, and Shorty groaned. Whether he went over to exorcise the inhabitants of Mrs. Smith's attic he never told us.

I'm sure, however, that he did go, because Mrs. Smith, still beset by someone in her attic, changed her approach. She would phone either the switchboard or the power company office, depending on the time of day, and announce mysteriously, "Tell Mr. Gammel there is raspberry pie." I think she had found the right bait.

On some great days a crew of three or four linemen drove over from the main office at Kalispell, sixteen miles away, for a special job — to extend a power line, for instance. They were fine fellows who clanked as Shorty did, because they wore the same equipment, and they swaggered a little, as they had a right to do. I remember telling one of them, with honest admiration, "You look so picturesque!" He barked a laugh and answered, "Humoresque is more like it."

When they were visiting, Mr. Tills made a special effort to put down poor Shorty, calling him a grunt instead of a lineman, and making it clear that he was afraid to get off

119

the ground by climbing. But the visiting crew treated Shorty as one of their own, with an occasional glance at Mr. Tills that could have been translated, "Buster, with all the lard you carry around, you *couldn't* get off the ground!"

I had been gone from Whitefish for many years when Shorty died. Someone sent me a newspaper clipping about his death and funeral. I remember reading that there had been a funeral procession down Central Avenue and thinking that his laughing spirit must have enjoyed it. There was nothing he liked better than a parade, unless it was the annual Firemen's Ball.

In 1977, I began a serious search for facts about Shorty's funeral, and a strange thing happened. I found that he had been forgotten almost completely in a town where he used to be better known than the mayor, the chief of police or even the oldest pioneer settlers. A very few people remembered Shorty, but there was no written record of him in Whitefish at all!

A man past middle-age told me, "Sure, I remember him. He used to give us kids small change when he had any. He liked us."

Marguerite Cole Moomaw, who lives in Nebraska now, was a telephone girl when I was. She remembers that Shorty helped her when she was scared. For a while, one of the jobs the girl on evening shift had to do was to go to the dim and cavernous back room of the power company's building and turn on the street lights. This involved pulling two plugs, as long as your arm, out of sockets and putting them into other sockets, meanwhile worrying about how many calls were coming in, unanswered, on the switchboard.

Turning on the street lights never scared me, but Mar-

120

guerite says she still has nightmares about it. If Shorty was around, he took care of the street lights for her, and she is still grateful.

Dick Adams, who was publisher of the weekly *Whitefish Pilot* in 1977, had never met Shorty, but did his best to dig up information for me. He checked the Volunteer Fire Department's records and the City Clerk's cemetery records and even telephoned the Flathead County Clerk in Kalispell — and couldn't find a thing. He ran across a couple of old-timers who vaguely recalled someone name Gambrel, but that's not Gammel. The undertaker had moved away, taking his records with him. The power company had changed ownership a couple of times.

Art Engelter of Whitefish said he thought Shorty died early in the fall of 1940; he had the date in mind because his own father died then and Art, back at work at the Great Northern depot, helped load Shorty's body on a train for shipment to Virginia.

Now I had a tentative date to go by. I wrote to the Bureau of Records and Statistics in Helena. They said Vernon Gammel died October 23, 1940, at Whitefish and gave me the reference number for his death certificate.

Then Brian Cockhill, archivist at the Montana Historical Society, looked up the *Whitefish Pilot* for appropriate dates and sent me photocopies of two stories. (The *Pilot* itself doesn't have complete files on old issues.)

Shorty would have been pleased with the fuss the town made over his funeral. (I can't imagine him hovering over the proceedings, though. He really did hate to get off the ground.) "The chapel was filled to capacity with friends of the deceased," the *Pilot* reported. Mourners included his co-workers at the Mountain States Power Company, members of the Spanish-American War Veterans Organi-

121

zation, representatives of Lion Mountain Post 276 of Veterans of Foreign Wars, the Benevolent and Protective Order of Elks, the Whitefish Rotary Club and the Volunteer Fire Department. A. B. Horstmann from Bigfork, an old friend and a former Whitefish postmaster, represented the power company.

I doubt whether Shorty ever went to church except to buy a good supper cooked by the church ladies, but an Episcopal minister preached at his funeral, and two church ladies provided suitable music.

"The body lay in state after the service until the afternoon," the *Pilot* said. Good. That was only proper. Then, "the flag-draped casket was removed from the funeral home and placed in the fire truck, escorted by members of the department." That's just as it should have been. Shorty had been fire chief for years, making the firemen practice where the hydrants ain't.

"With the Lion Mountain Post colors and the American flag borne at the head of the procession of Veterans of Foreign Wars, comrades of the Spanish-American War, the City Fire Department and a group of citizens, the body was removed to the Great Northern station where the last services for the dead were given by Lion Mountain Post. As the body was placed aboard the Empire Builder on its way to its home in Hampton, Virginia, a firing squad gave the last salute and taps were sounded."

Shorty didn't travel alone. "The body was accompanied to Hampton by C. P. Young, Spanish-American War veteran and member of Lion Mountain Post." And back in Virginia there was another military funeral before Vernon Gammel was buried in the family plot with his parents.

Strange to say, that was his second trip home in a short

122

period of time. Shorty had recently attended a national convention of Spanish-American veterans in Detroit and visited the World's Fair in New York. Then he went to Hampton for the first time in forty years and got acquainted with his brothers and their wives and children. He took sick soon after he returned to Whitefish and died in the Whitefish Hospital.

He was born February 7, 1876, and died at age 64. He went to work for Mountain States Power Company in 1909; he worked at Polson before moving to Whitefish.

I remember Shorty fondly. He was a clown who loved to laugh and to be laughed at. He used to do a few steps of a dance that he called the cakewalk, and he taught me how to do them — an exercise that came close to dislocating the hip joints. He was kind to everybody. He got a lot out of life and put a lot into it, and in 1940 he left it. But thirty-seven years later, there was no record of him at all in Whitefish, and only a handful of people remembered his name. *Sic transit gloria* — thus passes the glory.

It is comforting to think that he no longer sleeps in the glare of an electric light that will wake him to panic if it goes out.

World Before Radio

    YOUNGSTERS DIDN'T DEMAND MUCH in the way of entertainment when I was growing up in Whitefish. We didn't fret about ways to fill up time, because there was little of it to spare. Grownups worked very long hours, and kids went to school from nine to four with an hour and quarter off for dinner. (Call it lunch if you want to, but we didn't.) We didn't go home even at four if we were caught doing something forbidden. It takes quite a while to write "I must not chew gum in school" 100 times. After school there was kindling to split and firewood to carry in and snow to shovel. So we all kept fairly busy, and just getting your cold, wet feet dry by the stove without scorching your shoes was entertainment of a kind. At least it was a challenge.

    Our world was quiet. Music came only when invited;

124

you had to do more than flip a switch. If you had a phonograph, usually called a *victor-ola*, it played one short-term record at a time and you wound it carefully before each record and also put in a new needle. Then you sat back and listened. What you got was not just background decibels to do something else by. It was something you wanted to hear.

There was, of course, music heard in passing: Evelyn Stacey practicing her piano lesson, some big boy's slide trombone moaning because he was in the Whitefish Boys Band, or a railroad man called Scotty, who was determined to learn to play the bagpipes and marched all over town doing it because you can't play the pipes while sitting still at home.

Most of our entertainment was home talent (to use the word loosely), but I realize now that we had a few resident performers who were too good for us. Mrs. Bernard was one. She was a handsome blonde lady who often appeared on stage at public gatherings in the Masonic Temple, wearing a satin dress with a small train. She was much in demand for vocal solos, and she sang the national anthem whenever it was needed. (There used to be some disagreement about what the national anthem *was*: opinion divided about 50-50 between "The Star-Spangled Banner" and "My County 'Tis of Thee.")

Our elders whispered behind their hands that Mrs. Bernard had a Trained Voice, and she did indeed sound a lot different from the ladies in the church choir. But we little Philistines who had never heard classical music sung by a professional thought she was hilarious. She must have been lonely amid the alien corn. She was too good for the likes of us, and I wish I could tell her so.

One kind of entertainment that drew a good house in

our town was any church's Christmas program. The first time I took part, a few days after my eighth birthday, I was in a line of wiggling little girls who sang. They all swayed in unison except me, the new girl in town. First the child on my left would bump me, then the child on my right. I glared and stood like a rock. Nobody had told me to sway. Nobody had told them either, this time, but their act the year before had required it, and they still thought they ought to do it that way, every Christmas until the end of the world.

I used to pass the time between acts by staring up at the stove pipe. Before our church had a basement and a furnace, the building was heated with a big wood-burning stove that was quite far from the chimney. They were tenuously connected with yards and yards of black stove-pipe, and it was interesting to calculate which members of the enraptured audience were in the best position to get a lap full of soot if the pipe fell down.

Just going downtown on Saturday night to do some trading was entertainment. What was called trading then is what we call shopping now. No matter how it sounds, it didn't involve exchanging beaver plews for Green River knives. The medium of exchange was ordinary money, except that anybody who was anybody charged every-thing to an account that was settled once a month, on payday. If you did your trading in cash, it was because your credit was no good.

Saturday night trading expeditions involved whole families, even though only one member might be needing a major investment, like shoes or a coat. Kids went along gladly because there was always the chance that the father of the family might end the evening by treating his little flock to cones at Mr. Matthews' ice cream parlor. Whitefish was festive on Saturday night, with people buying groceries, fingering merchandise they wished they could afford and socializing with chance-met friends.

That was before you pushed a wire cart, helped yourself off the shelves and paid cash at the checkout stand. The old way was more personal. You told Mr. Cooke or Mr. Crum (depending on whose store you patronized) what you wanted, and he reached up behind him and brought it down and scribbled on a charge slip. Grocers had worse handwriting than doctors. When the lady of the house tried to check those slips against the monthly statement, she got pretty frustrated. She knew very well she had never bought 3 tm pfw in her whole life. She wouldn't have known how to cook it.

More formal entertainments, connected with school or church, were frequent. Recitations were much in demand at public gatherings. Miss Jessica Reed, who taught high school English, was great at this. She could be three or four people all at once and furthermore do it in memorized prose, which is harder to learn than poetry, and with appropriate gestures. When Miss Reed did it, the number was called a reading. When kids did it, we spoke a piece.

Almost any child could speak a piece on short notice. We did a lot of memorizing, some of it voluntary. The other day a friend of mine remarked, *a propos* of nothing:

Lars Porsena of Clusium, by the Nine Gods he swore
That the great house of Tarquin should suffer wrong
no more.

To which I responded,

> By the Nine Gods he swore it, and named a
> trysting-day,
> And bade his messengers ride forth, east and west
> and south and north to summon his array.

We, my friend and I, are of the generation that loved the excitement of *Horatius at the Bridge* and memorized miles of it, just for fun, "O Tiber! Father Tiber! to whom the Romans pray, A Roman's life, a Roman's arms, take thou in charge this day!"

Nobody had told us that the world would end not with a bang, but a whimper. We grew up admiring bangs and clashes and fights against hopeless odds, with no whimpers. When brave Horatius, the captain of the gate, wounded and wearing his armor, made it safely to shore, even the enemy cheered. We believed that Sir Galahad's strength was as the strength of ten because his heart was pure, and if we ourselves were pretty feeble it must be because we had done something naughty.

One of my most acclaimed efforts was *The Burial of Moses*. I thought people applauded because I did it so well. Now I suspect it was the lisp that fascinated them:

> By Nebo'th lonely mountain, on thith thide
> Jordan'th wave,
> In a vale in the land of Moab there lieth a lonely
> grave.
> And no man knowth that thepulchre and no man
> thaw it e'er,
> For the angelth of God upturned the thod and laid
> the dead man there.

It goes on for miles.

Too bad memorizing has gone out of style. I can still draw, for my own pleasure, on an endless treasure of poetry and Bible verses, do the Gettysburg Address for a typing exercise, and show off with "Twinkle, twinkle, little star" in Latin.

Small localized entertainments took place; in grade school there was a ritual known as a peanut shower. If a class liked its teacher, some brave kid confided in the teacher in the next room: Would she please call Miss Tobias out on some pretext late Friday afternoon? She obliged, and when Miss Tobias came back, she was pelted with peanuts in their shells. She expressed astonishment and delight at being so honored, and the class laughed and shrieked and ate the peanuts. I never noticed whether the guest of honor got any. The janitor must have hated us.

Dramatic offerings consisted of high school plays, staged at the Orpheum The-ay-ter. Virtually nobody had ever seen a professional cast at work, so standards weren't awfully high. The height of praise was, "They sure learned their parts good."

The English teacher, who was also the drama coach, was restricted in her choice of plays by the fact that very few boys were available. Girls were not very convincing in male roles, so we stayed with comedy. The Orpheum stage had drawbacks. Once, as a gabby maiden aunt, I was to enter a garden arm in arm with the ingenue, but the curtain rose with us on opposite sides of the stage and nothing to hide behind while one sneaked across the back. I beckoned wildly, and we stepped forward, each from her own side, to meet center stage as I caroled, "Ah, theah you ah, my deah!" in high-society accents. Our coach must have died twice over while waiting for that brilliant improvisation.

Big kids (this was before teen-agers were discovered) occasionally passed some spare time around the big Victrola at Mr. Haines's drugstore, pretending they were thinking of buying a record. This didn't fool Mr. Haines for a minute. No kid ever had money to waste on a record. But he played along for a reasonable length of time before telling us tactfully that maybe we ought to go do something else.

In high school we encountered an institution called Literary Society. Entertainment it was not, although maybe it was supposed to be. The school administration made no attempt to sell the idea to the student body. Literary Society was just plain required. Twice a year every last one of us in Whitefish High School — about a hundred, maybe a few more — had to get up in front of all the rest and suffer publicly through a personal appearance that was sometimes as hard on the audience as it was on the unwilling performer. We had to do it to pass English, and we had to pass English to graduate.

Literary Society was divided into the Alphas and the Thetas. Perhaps it was hoped that lively competition would result and make everyone eager to participate. It didn't work out that way. Everybody I knew hated both Alpha and Theta with a total lack of prejudice.

Literary Society wasn't necessarily literary. A girl who played the piano could fulfill her obligation with a solo. The rest of us envied the piano players because they performed with their backs to the audience. A kid could recite something memorized or participate in a group musical presentation or appear in a theoretically comical skit on the stage. We never knew where those silly little dramas came from, but any fool could tell they weren't literature. A boy who was paralyzed by the idea of doing *anything* might get off with writing an extra theme and mumbling it down his shirt front while the rest of us suffered with him.

Once a girl named Susan (or was it Mavis?) surprised everybody by reading a long romantic poem that she had written herself. This went over well with everybody but me. I was jealous as hell. *I* was the one who wrote poetry around there; everybody knew that. And here was this rank amateur, with no reputation for being smiled upon by the Muse, stealing my thunder!

Next time my turn came to do or die for Alpha, naturally I approached the teachers with the suggestion that if a poetry reading of one's own work was desirable, I'd be glad to contribute. I would write something special and recite it from memory. But the teacher felt that Susan's offering was all that was needed along that line.

Instead, I was one of the ham actors in a corny little skit involving such characters as never lived on land or sea. I was Squire somebody, a bucolic party wearing overalls, with an empty corncob pipe between my teeth.

Possibly this mass agony was supposed to prepare us to take our place in civilized society and speak on our feet glibly, helping the nation to advance. What it really did was to convince us that we wanted no part of public life whatever.

There was one way to evade the Alphas and the Thetas. That was to make the debating team. I took this way out my last two years in high school. The three girls on our team learned more than we ever wanted to know about compulsory arbitration of labor disputes and whether Orientals should have the right to become U.S. citizens.

Once Whitefish debated Shelby, and neither school could afford to send the team all the way to the other town, so we met in Browning before an audience composed almost entirely of Blackfeet Indians. One of our team members missed the train, leaving only two of us, Audrey Deighton and me, to face three young geniuses from Shelby. We were awfully scared. I picked out a motherly-looking Blackfeet lady in the front row and orated directly to her because she kept smiling as if she hoped our side would win. Her obvious good will kept me from collapsing. And after all that tension, I don't remember which school won the debate.

Movies were the one entertainment gift from the outside world that we could depend on. The Orpheum The-ay-ter had one every night, plus a Saturday matinee. They were, of course, silent movies except that quite a lot of people read the subtitles aloud: "In a vine-covered cottage dwelt a maiden fair," and there was Lillian Gish. "Drop that pistol!" and there, steely-eyed and thin of lip, was William S. Hart.

Mr. Sissel owned the theater, took the tickets, and I think ran the projector. Mrs. Sissel manned the box-office and provided the piano accompaniment — sweet, soft tinklings for love scenes, violent thumping for the U.S. Cavalry galloping to save a wagon train.

My mother had a pass good for every night, courtesy of the management, because she was City Treasurer. Thus I should have been a steady customer, but we had a rule at our house: no more than one show a week. Probably the purpose was to strengthen my character through deprivation.

That was before double features; we got one main feature, one short custard-pie-type comedy, maybe a travelogue with the last subtitle reading, "And so we sail into the sunset, leaving beautiful Madagascar," Coming Attractions and slides advertising local emporia. There was

132

also a cracked glass slide that came on several times; it admonished the audience to be patient while the operator was changing the reel.

The most spectacular movie I remember was *A Daughter of the Gods*, starring Annette Kellerman doing her celebrated sixty-foot dive, or maybe it was eighty. Word got around that she did it in the nude, which was the genteel way of saying stark naked. Hardly anyone believed that, but the turnout was tremendous. The primmest, godliest people in town flocked to that show, because how could they complain unless they saw it with their own eyes?

The dive was, after all, disappointing. The star sped along the far side of some bushes and dived, all right, but she moved so fast that, no matter how hard you squinted, you couldn't tell whether she was naked or not. There should have been an instant replay.

I was small enough to believe everything I saw when Mary Pickford came along in a romantic tidbit called *Hearts Adrift*. There was this girl all by herself on an island, see, she'd been shipwrecked or something, and her only companion was her pet wolf, see. Then a man was washed up on shore and she had a baby — but how could she when there was no preacher to marry them? — and he went away and she jumped into a convenient volcano with the baby in her arms.

I wept buckets of tears and was not entirely consoled when my mother assured me that little Mary didn't jump into a real volcano but would be back in other movies. When Mary Pickford and I were about thirty-five years older, I had lunch with her in New York and was gratified to note that the volcano hadn't left any scars. The lunch was arranged by my agent, who thought I should help her

133

write her autobiography.

Later I interviewed her at her apartment, trying to believe it was really the Johnson kid from Whitefish who was following Mary Pickford around for a look at the family photographs. I moved back to Montana before anything came of the book idea, and someone else helped her write it.

From the great outside world Whitefish received, in addition to movies, Chautauqua in summer, Lyceum in winter, and almost nothing else. But once a carnival came to town, and local housewives took the wash off the line so it wouldn't be stolen. No doubt this was prudent, but why would those beautiful visitors, the painted ladies and the swaggering men, want a bunch of well-worn diapers or a locomotive fireman's longjohns?

The carnival had to have a city license, and when the manager arranged this with my mother he buttered up everybody in City Hall, especially the police, by handing out passes. With my mother's pass in hand, I became the carnival's best customer. Ah, the wonders! — and all for free. Three times I shuddered happily at the snake charmer's booth, twice I stood breathless while the daredevil death-defying motorcyclists whirled around in their wooden pit, and I rode the merry-go-round something like eighty times.

Chautauqua was five days of concentrated culture, including inspirational lectures, all kinds of musical and dramatic performances, and acts that, under less elevated sponsorship, would have been vaudeville. All this took place in a big gray tent, with the audience sitting on benches built of planks and trying to keep cool by waving palm-leaf fans.

Chautauqua held forth both afternoon and evening,

134

and I had to attend every performance to which a season ticket entitled me. My mother had a high opinion of culture, and I wasn't really opposed, but Chautauqua came during our all-too-short swimming season, when any sensible kid wanted to be over at Whitefish Lake.

For children there was even morning activity, rehearsing for a big song-and-dance performance by the local small fry at the end of the five days. I got roped into this just once. The harried lady who rehearsed us found out soon enough that the little Johnson girl couldn't carry a tune, so she tactfully diverted me to something called the Dance of the Russian Snowflakes. When she realized — as I already had — that I didn't qualify for that either, we parted by mutual consent, without recriminations.

Lyceum was even more cultural. It came to the high school auditorium for an occasional evening performance during the winter. Lyceum attracted the intelligentsia. It featured chalk talks, travel lectures and stuff like that. The only performance I can remember was yodeling by a Swiss family. For quite a while after that you could hear strangled attempts at yodeling all over town.

In spite of this breathless round of entertainment, sometimes there just wasn't anything to do. On a lazy Sunday afternoon, one could take part in the time-honored ceremony of Walking Down to the Post Office. If, on the way, I stopped in and picked up Marguerite Cole, we giggled all the way. Girls in their early teens do giggle, and anyway we were accomplices in a little smuggling operation. The contraband was books. Her father had some of the Tarzan books, also *She* by H. Rider Haggard. My mother didn't want me to read such stuff, but books were scarce, there was no public library, and I had already been through all ours two or three times. So Marguerite got me *She* and a bunch of Tarzans and I hid them under the front steps at home.

When we were sophomores, our Sunday giggling was close to hysteria, because on Monday we had to go back to school and fight Julius Caesar. We were home from the Gallic Wars only on a weekend pass. We two were the entire class in Latin II. Ranged against us trembling recruits were Caesar and his legions, backed by Miss Robertson, who was always on his side.

To get back to the post office: one did not get there with the expectation of finding any mail. It was just a goal. If Marguerite wasn't available, I strolled alone and dreamed. Something marvelous might be waiting at the post office. Even when Box 41 was obviously empty, I turned the little knob to the remembered combination and slid my hand in to make sure the emptiness wasn't an optical illusion. Ah, well, maybe next time. The letters that might have come were wonderful. Like this:

"We read your poem in your school paper with profound admiration, and we are going to print it in our magazine. Our check for $100 is enclosed. ($100 was the largest sum I could imagine.) We want to publish everything you write from now on forever."

Or ardent letters from an unknown admirer, either a duke or a misunderstood outlaw, who didn't sign his name because he felt he wasn't worthy. Or notification that I was the heiress to vast estates in England, where my Grandpa Barlow came from. (He wasn't heir to anything.) Or just a kindly reassurance that I did have talent as a basketball player and it wasn't my fault when the ball hit me square in the face and knocked my glasses off.

None of those dreams-of-glory letters came, but I remember fondly the ritual of going down to the post office,

136

and I recommend dreaming.

Because some dreams come true, even more abundantly than the dreamer had hoped. This has happened to me, and I still can't quite believe it. Although long ago I gave up poetry in favor of prose, no editor has yet expressed a wish to publish *everything* I write. Still, the score isn't bad.

In Whitefish, with its simple pleasures, we lived in a quiet, cozy isolated little world. When we began to hear about radio (or raddio, as some people preferred to pronounce it), we had no inkling of how much this complicated curiosity was going to change our lives.

Magazines began to publish directions for making a crystal set to receive broadcasts. You started by winding a lot of copper wire around a Quaker Oats box, and that was where I stopped, too. There was nothing to receive on a crystal set except Morse code from a sending set that the Dugan boys had concocted, and I wasn't going to learn Morse.

A man over at the lake bought a really powerful, expensive receiving set with lots of vacuum tubes. He could get programs from far away if the weather was just right. If it wasn't, he got static. His set had a speaker horn like a Victrola.

About 1923 I pried myself loose from twenty dollars and bought a secondhand two-tube set with earphones, three dials, and a lot of batteries that stood on the floor and had to be wired up exactly right. Getting anything other than squeals and howls depended on luck and twisting those dials around.

There was no broadcasting station within hundreds of miles, so nobody was choosy about programs. What everybody wanted was distance. I was delighted with a

137

lecture on raising baby chickens emanating from Omaha; sometimes Pittsburgh came in loud and clear (or anyway clear); once I even got Schenectady, New York. It was customary for the triumphant listener to write a post card to the far-away station with the good news: "I heard you last night just fine at 8:45," and for the station to acknowledge this gratefully.

More broadcasting stations were established. Then there were networks. An unbelievable prophecy, that sometime you could ditch that herd of big batteries and simply plug into an electric connection, came true. There was competition among broadcasters, and listeners could pick and choose their programs.

Everybody, all over, could listen to the same demagogues, howl at the same comedians, make a fad of the same new slang. Everybody with a radio — no longer called a receiving set — suddenly was sophisticated, part of the great outside world. So why should small towns provide their own amateur entertainment when professonals could do it better and the audience didn't even have to leave home?

Whitefish used to have some real characters. They had to struggle to survive as characters after the radio professionals took over, with teams of highly paid people to write their dialogue.

Listeners became addicts, so accustomed to having sounds of any old kind coming into the house that they were nervous when it was quiet. It was easier to leave the radio on and not listen than to bear the unaccustomed silence. For better or worse, the quiet, the isolation, the parochialism were gone.

People used to make their own music. They stood around a piano or, more likely, an old-fashioned pump

138

organ, and sang just because they enjoyed it—cold sober, too. We had an organ, and my father played it. He also liked to sing. Once he invited me to join him in a hymn I knew very well. I piped up with a will, and he turned and gave me a sad, sad look.

Because I could not then, and cannot now, carry a tune. (A few years later a psychology professor sighed, "You don't test tone deaf. You're more tone hard-of-hearing." The bewildered expression on his face made me suspect I had set back Psychology 102 about fifty years.)

I still feel guilty about disappointing my father. It happened again every time school report cards came out. I was on the honor roll, but only second or third. He couldn't understand why his daughter wasn't first, and he mentioned it. I couldn't explain it but developed the conviction that I was one of the world's born losers. Failures flatten me but they are never a surprise. Successes throw me off balance. My father didn't live long enough to get much satisfaction out of *them.*

One formerly important activity that has lately fallen on hard times requires just one person, a pencil and a piece of blank paper. People actually sat down and wrote letters to relatives, friends and sweethearts. A later generation finds this too time-consuming, or itself insufficiently literate, and simply reaches for the telephone. When letter writing went out of style, we lost something. A box of old letters could be read again and again years later with delight or sadness, especially if they began "My darling" and were tied with faded ribbon. What kind of sentimental charm is there in a bunch of paid telephone bills?

My mother often nagged me about answering letters from Grandma Johnson, who wrote in a crabbed hand that I couldn't figure out: she never said anything interesting anyway. Not that my mother was fond of her mother-in-law, a tactless old lady who once acknowledged a photograph of me by saying, "She looks like you but is a sweet-looking child just the same." (Actually, I looked like a juvenile version of Grandma — big noses ran on *her* side of the family.) I just didn't have anything to say to Grandma. My memories of her were intimidating. When she lived with us during my early years, she showed me Grandpa's glass eye, which she kept, in loving memory, in a drawer in her bedside table.

But people wrote letters. Also they talked, and nobody said, "Oh, be quiet — I'm watching television." It hadn't been invented. At our house we talked for fun and information and to pass the time while doing small, tedious chores. My mother passed on to me the family jokes about how her two sisters tried to get out of scouring burned kettles and other matters that were ours alone. Like the story about the stingy farm woman back in Iowa who never cooked quite enough for either her own family or company dinner. Naturally, there were never any leftovers, and she always said with beaming complacency, looking at the empty plates, 'There, just all and just enough!''

She told me about the annual flood in McGregor, when the main street almost washed down into the Mississippi River. And about teaching country school at sixteen to kids older and bigger than she was, who had scared out their last two men teachers. They did it by talking Norwegian. My mother's father came from England, her mother from Norway, but all the new teacher could say in Norwegian was "Good morning, it's a nice day today." So she said it on the first day of school — and never had a bit of trouble with those big roughnecks.

Her best stories were about Virgin Em back in

140

McGregor. This lady had been married eight or nine times — maybe she had kept track, but other people had to guess. One of her husbands was named Van Sickle, and that was the name she used when my mother was a girl. Emma Van Sickle had her own private graveyard, with all her late husbands in it except one rascal who had been hanged somewhere, the story went, and on each grave a wooden headboard with a name or initials on it. But Clinton Van Sickle had been very dear to her, and his grave had a marble monument with this inscription:

> Clinty, my heart clings to thee, love.
> In Heaven I hope to meet above.
> You was ever kind and true to me
> So was I to you. Emma G. V.

He must have been quite a man, to stand out like that in a crowd!

My mother said Virgin Em's place was on a hill, and everybody in town knew when she'd had a fight with her current husband, because then the head boards shone whiter in the sun. In short, she won all the arguments, and she disciplined the old man by sending him out to whitewash the headboards of his predecessors.

That's part of the heritage of laughter that my mother passed on to me while we washed dishes or shelled peas.

The Glacier Obsession

A funny story about Glacier National Park concerns the visit of the famous author, Mary Roberts Rinehart, in 1917, when the Park was in its infancy. (It was established in 1910). The mountains and glaciers had been there a long time, but the national park hadn't. The Rinehart party traveled in style, with the famous Eaton guides, packers and horses. There was champagne, too, and what is more, the famous lady wrote a book about the trip. It was entitled *Tenting Tonight,* and it brought the area to the attention of a lot of people who hadn't heard about it before.

One night, while getting ready for bed in her tent, the celebrated lady author punctured her air mattress with a hatpin. That's all there is to the story, but it gets funnier with the passage of time. A hatpin? What on earth was she

142

doing with a hatpin on a camping trip? Did she plan to use it to defend herself from bears? No, in those days ladies always wore hats and did their hair high, and it took a couple of hatpins to keep the hat anchored. At the time it happened, a lot of slightly jealous people who weren't rich enough to travel with an air mattress laughed merrily and figured that small accident served an Eastern dude just about right.

My first experiences with social strata, rich people and Eastern dudes, were all in Glacier Park. We unrich Westerners were suspicious of the whole lot of them. We looked down on them because we thought they looked down on us. But they didn't even *see* us, which made the situation even more irritating. Years later, when I lived in a big Eastern city, I learned not to see strangers; it is a necessary protective device where there are too many people. But in the uncrowded West, in *my* country, it's bad manners, and on the trail it's proper to acknowledge the existence of other human beings by saying hello.

My early memories of Glacier National Park, whose western entrance is some twenty-six miles from Whitefish, are less about the breath-taking mountain scenery than about the vast social chasm between Eastern dudes and us who lived around there. We were especially doubtful of famous people. For outdoor wear, rich Easterners were costumed by Abercrombie and Fitch or the equivalent.

Once, trudging along a trail, some of us met Irvin S. Cobb. We loved his stories in the *Saturday Evening Post,* but that was *his* world; what was he doing in ours? (There was no mistaking him; he was the homeliest man I ever saw, with a face like a frog).

Mr. Cobb was carrying fishing equipment, and his shirt and pants had well-pressed creases instead of wrinkles. He wore high laced boots of off-white leather. Those boots endeared him to us. They were scratched and worn and water-stained. They had taken him through rough country and into mountain streams. We knew right away that this was no dude. We judged that even though he was an Easterner and world-famous, Irvin S. Cobb was acceptable in our world. In Western slang, he'd do to ride the river with.

All this was long before you could drive casually through Glacier Park on your way to somewhere else. You couldn't drive casually *anywhere* in western Montana then; the roads were too bad, where they existed at all.

So Park visitors, including us locals, went by train, and since the journey was expensive, those from far away tended to settle down and stay for several weeks at one or more of the hotels, which the Great Northern Railway owned. This was a sensible arrangement. The railroad generated a lot of summer passenger traffic by promoting Glacier as an unspoiled playground full of scenic wonders and, having got the dudes out there, provided food and lodging on which, presumably, it also made a profit. The temporary hotel help was recruited from the University of Minnesota.

By 1960, most people no longer came by train, so in December of that year the Great Northern sold its hostelries to Donald Hummel, a businessman of Tucson, Arizona. He operated them under the name of Glacier Park, Inc. (A couple of years after that I got into an argument with a fiesty lady about who owned those hotels. I couldn't convince her that they had changed hands. What she knew, she knew, and she couldn't bear contradiction. The funny thing about this argument was that it took place in Tangiers, Morocco, while we were eating cous-cous in the elegant Rif Hotel. This just goes to show that some tourists will fight about anything anywhere. She wouldn't speak to me for the rest of the tour, all the way back to Madrid).

Back in the days when East was East and West was West and the twain met briefly and suspiciously in Glacier Park, we went from Whitefish to Belton (now West Glacier) on the train, in hiking clothes and carrying our possessions in back-packs. Lots of people back-pack there now; it is the "in" thing to do. But in my time it wasn't fashionable — it just showed that we couldn't afford to stay or eat at the Lewis Hotel, now called Lake McDonald Lodge.

From Belton we walked to Apgar and there boarded a big motorboat that took us to the hotel at the head of Lake McDonald. If we were really economizing, we hiked all the way — about ten miles. There was a road that far.

Then we roughed it, and most of what we did was probably illegal, but the statute of limitations must have expired since then, so it's all right to confess it now. There may have been some campgrounds; I don't remember them. I do remember that one rainy night five of us, including my mother, crawled into a barn that had a loose board on the back and slept on the hay. We all slid during the night, and the roof leaked, so we woke up in the morning at the bottom of the hay pile with our feet in a puddle.

Another night we managed to get into a dance pavilion and slept on the hard floor. I had contracted a bad sunburn three or four days before by floating around on a raft on Whitefish Lake all one lovely afternoon. The burn was beginning to peel, the straps of my pack had rubbed some skin off my shoulders, and when I complained about having the equivalent of stand-up fish scales on my back, some wag in the party suggested that I was no doubt sprouting wings and a little discomfort was only to be expected, as when a baby gets a new tooth.

We weren't supposed to sleep where we slept or to cook where we cooked, but we were fairly experienced woodsmen, and we didn't get caught. We used wood that was already down and dead, and we were experts at completely extinguishing our little cooking fires. (Some thirty years later, using a modern portable gasoline stove at a modern, legal campground, I came close to setting Glacier National Park afire, but that's a later story). Once we found a huge edible mushroom of the puffball type, sliced it and fried it like steak — it made a fine meal for the whole bunch of us.

Being curious about how the rich dudes from the East fared at the hotel, a couple of us peered through a dining room window one night. Some of those ladies wore low-topped, long-skirted *satin* evening dresses! Out in the wilderness, mind you, roughing it in the Rocky Mountains! Ah, the hardships suffered by the daring adventurers who spent the summer in Glacier National Park, instead of back in Newport where things were civilized.

Some of them did have great adventures and were out-going enough to admit it. One day, a middle-aged woman in an elegant hiking costume came running out to the boat dock at the hotel calling, "Cahl! Cahl!"

A young man who was about to go swimming answered, "Yes, Mothah?" (Translating this cleverly from Eastern to Western dialect, I figured out that his name was Carl and hers was Mother. We treat the letter R with more respect). Mothah was simply ecstatic — she had picked half a pint of huckleberries growing wild in the woods. Cahl was polite about it.

146

Meanwhile I watched to see how Cahl would react when he hit that water; I had just got out of it, regretting having got in, and was trying (while my teeth chattered) to understand how water that cold could remain fluid. It was liquid glaciers.

I rather expected that Cahl, being a dude, would collapse when he hit that cold water and would probably never come up. But he emerged in a thrashing crawl and swam clear around the dock to prove he could do it — and maybe because people were watching. I began to suspect that "Easterner" was not synonymous with "softy." He didn't go in again, though. Neither did I.

Next day (after sleeping on that dance pavilion floor) our hardy little band set out for Sperry Chalet. The rich went on horses, with a guide. We went on foot, six miles that seemed straight up. We grew thirstier and thirstier, and nobody had had the wits to bring a canteen. Most of the way we were tormented by the sound of rushing water — nice cold water in vast quantities, gushing through a narrow stream bed down below at our right, not far away but totally inaccessible. Between us and it there was a vertical drop down a cliff. We chose to go thirsty rather than court disaster by trying to get a drink. And somewhere along the way I got mad.

"I don't want to see Sperry Glacier," I announced bitterly. "I don't give a hang about *any* glacier. I am going to stay right here and enjoy my sunburn and listen to the creek and be thirsty, and you can pick me up on your way back. Good-bye."

And there I stayed, and on they went after some argument. They were gone for some hours. They didn't reach the glacier, 9.9 miles from the Lewis Hotel, but they did get to Sperry Chalet and brought back pictures to prove it.

147

I lay there propped against a log, stubborn as Achilles before the walls of Troy, and after a while the branches in a tree above me began to look mighty like a bobcat or perhaps a small mountain lion. I didn't move. I was the prototype of the petulant teenager. Let him leap, I thought. And will they be sorry when they find my blood and bones scattered all over the trail! The big cat dissolved into tree branches.

After an endless time, my companions returned, limping, but acting as if they had enjoyed the trip, which only made me madder. They had had a lovely drink of water up at the chalets — but they had also contracted some blisters in their boots. They had not tried to reach Sperry Glacier.

In those days, all respectable travelers going on a journey of any length took along a trunk as well as several pieces of hand luggage. It was in the Belton depot, while we waited for our train to return to Whitefish, that I first saw an example of that elegant contraption known as a wardrobe trunk. It had big and little drawers in it, very nice.

The pretty, well-dressed young lady who was fussing over it was weeping quietly, and to this day I wonder why. Had she had bad news from home — a death in the family, perhaps — that called her away from the splendors of lakes and mountain peaks? But surely in that case someone from among her friends at the hotel would have come this far with her for comfort. A girl in her early twenties wouldn't normally be at a resort hotel all alone. Had she impulsively and angrily left her husband back at the Lewis Hotel? She cried quietly as she tidied the lacy things in the drawers of her wardrobe trunk, waiting for the train. She was heartbreak, she was tragedy. Perhaps she was even disgrace. And I will never, never know either the beginning or the end of the story. I glimpsed only the middle of it,

148

more than fifty years ago.

I didn't see Glacier Park for a long time after graduating from the University of Montana in 1928. I worked in Okanogan, Washington, in Menasha, Wisconsin, in New York City. The cliff-hanger road along the Garden Wall, from the west side of the Park to the top, at Logan Pass, was finished in 1929. The whole of Going-to-the-Sun Highway, clear through to the east side, was opened in 1933.

I got a quick look at part of it in 1942, thanks to friends in Whitefish where I visited briefly, but I didn't really believe it. You could go all the way through in a car! Quite a lot of people were doing that, in spite of a war being on. And the most remarkable thing was that Easterners didn't look any different from Westerners any more, or act any different, either. You couldn't tell the difference until you heard them talk. (By that time I was accustomed to New York accents, from the Bronx to Park Avenue, and had met some New Yorkers who actually thought I talked funny. I still think that the counterman in a Manhattan hamburger stand was fooling when he let on that he couldn't understand my order for milk. How many ways can you pronounce *milk* in English, no matter where you're from?)

In the summer of 1952, my mother and I were living in Whitefish again. I had a longer look at the Park, in comfort, by car, for a whole week. My companion was Catherine A. Burnham (hereinafter known as Kay), a long-time friend and former neighbor in New York. I had visited her girlhood haunts in Massachusetts (no, no, haunts is not the right word — she is not a witch) where, no matter which way you look from the farm where she grew up, what you see belongs on a picture postcard. Now I was going to show her *our* picture postcard scenery.

149

She arrived in Whitefish by train. A couple of weeks earlier she had received the degree of Doctor of Philosophy from New York University. The title of her dissertation was "Reliability and Validity of Psychologists' Evaluation of Therapy Readiness," and for a few minutes, while she was explaining it, I almost understood what she was talking about.

This was my very first experience in vacationing by car. For the fifteen years I had worked in New York I didn't have or need one. We could take anything we might possibly want — how nice! How different from the miseries of back-packing years before! And I was pretty naive about the facilities available, in spite of having studied *Guide to Glacier National Park* by George C. Ruhle.

What I borrowed and packed would have taken us on an expedition into the Gobi Desert — bedding (never needed at the cabins and hotels we used), five gallons of gas (totally unnecessary), knapsacks, flannel shirts, winter pajamas (we did need them at Sperry), food, dishes, cooking equipment, a thermos bottle and a library: Mr. Ruhle's *Guide, Immortal Poems of the English Language,* and *How to Know the American Mammals.* The American mammals we met, mostly small rodents, seldom stood still long enough for us to find the right page in the book. A week before we reached Many Glacier, a ranger had shot a grizzly there, but it had been removed, and anyway if I meet a bear I won't need to look in a book to figure out that it's not a chipmunk.

The fact was that I didn't know any more about seeing Glacier Park by car than Kay did. But I drove, which made me captain, and Kay, who was a lieutenant in the Naval Reserve, was the crew. She dropped the anchor — every time we stopped on a grade, she leaped out and put a

150

chunk of rock where it would keep the car from rolling.

Glacier Park with roads and a car was a lot different from the way I remembered it way back then. And we were prosperous enough to buy our way under a roof every night — none of this sneaking into places where we weren't supposed to be. We traversed the cliff-hanging Going-to-the-Sun Highway along the Garden Wall, where Kay enjoyed the spectacular scenery — tall trees are so far below that they look like grass. (The only time I ever see the scenery up there is when someone else is driving). We made a short stop at Logan Pass, where there were facilities that a friend of mine called Going-to-the-John Chalet, enjoyed snowbanks and wild flowers, and rented a cabin at Rising Sun cabin camp.

We had no cooking facilities, so we unpacked our groceries at a public campground and undertook, with unwarranted self-confidence, to build a cooking fire. Wood was provided — in such big heavy chunks that we agreed a receding glacier must have left it there.

Our axe was ineffective, but we haggled off some bits, which Kay arranged hopefully in a stone fireplace while I unlimbered a one-burner gasoline stove as a backup device. The people who lent it to me had given me two lessons in operating it, but I flunked my final. I pumped the stove with great determination, held a match to it, and almost burned up Glacier National Park. The flame, which should have been short and blue, was tall and yellow. If anyone up in Alberta noticed northern lights to the south that evening, it was that flame they saw. After I knocked the stove off the log, the flame blazed horizontally. One thing I must say for that stove: even enveloped in fire, it didn't explode.

I went shrieking off to the nearest occupied campsite

and encountered a heroic fellow who raced back with me and tamed the stove. He even made Kay's wood fire burn — our frying pan of pork chops wasn't even warm. He was an awfully nice man, our rescuer. If I were a hot-shot reporter I would have found out more about him, but all I knew when the emergency was over was that he wore a red shirt and came from California.

Reading our little bunch of booklets about Glacier Park, I came upon the interesting fact that the mountains constituting its eastern edge had been folded up long ago and pushed some fifteen miles eastward out onto the prairie. The surface over which all this geology was pushed is known as the Lewis Overthrust. And this base, two booklets said, is "weak Cretaceous shale."

Now if there is one thing we need, it's a good solid foundation under great big mountains. Weak Cretaceous shale, indeed! We taxpayers have a right to expect something better than that. It was no use complaining to the Park rangers; they keep busy but they are not expected to build mountains. This looked like bureaucratic bungling on a high level. To get the facts straight before writing to my Congressman, I read further.

The Cretaceous period was part of the Mesozoic era, which began about 127,000,000 B.C., give or take a few million years. The Lewis Overthrust probably came early in the Eocene period of the Cenozoic era, maybe 58,000,000 B.C. So there was no use complaining to Washington. Criticizing the Power that was responsible might get me a chiding letter from the local Ministerial Association; the Vatican would ignore me. Anyway, if weak Cretaceous shale has held up those huge, handsome mountains all this time, they're probably safe to walk on.

From Rising Sun Cabin Camp we drove, mostly

through a hard rainstorm, to Waterton Lakes in Canada. Goodness, a foreign country! Both of us have been to a lot of foreign countries since then, but in 1952 we hadn't. We had an idea that crossing the border would be a pompous, official performance in which we would be required to spread all our belongings, from tooth brushes to coffee pot, in the road while customs officers looked severe. No such thing. All they wanted to know was whether we carried anything expensive, like cameras, and when we were coming back. They seemed glad to see us and hoped we'd have a nice time.

We didn't even have to show our identification. Kay was prepared to prove that she was an officer in the U.S. Navy, and I had an old New York pistol permit with a picture on it that made me look like an unrepentant multiple murderer.

We found a dandy cabin at Waterton with two bedrooms, excellent cooking and heating facilities, and lots of hot water. The only thing wrong with it was that every time we left it we lost it. I have a knack for forgetting names. (I once beamingly introduced as Mr. Nichols a man whose name was Rosenberg.) Trying to get back to our cabin camp, I assured Kay that the name of our landlord was either Kennedy or Seely. It was Reeves. We wrote that down in our log so we wouldn't go looking for McGillicuddy or Robertson next time.

Every time we ventured downtown, we lost our happy home. Trying to find it by using a large mud puddle as a landmark didn't work; other puddles appeared as the rain continued. So we agreed that I would just drive the car and that Kay would decide which way to go. Thus she was promoted from crew to navigator, more in keeping with her Navy rank, and we had no more trouble because she used a large fence as a landmark. It was more dependable than mud puddles.

Next day the rain stopped, so we took a boat ride, which was what we were there for. During part of the ride, we were back in Montana, having crossed the invisible border by boat.

We enjoyed the scenery and were impressed by the virulent camera fever from which some of our fellow passengers were suffering. The only way they ever saw anything was through a view finder. One man was loaded down with three cameras and his wife had two. They spoke to nobody but each other, and then only to discuss which filter to use. Another man had been traveling for six weeks, had used thirty rolls of movie film and couldn't remember which states he took them in.

Getting out of Canada was as easy as getting in. We dutifully reported that we had bought two neckties, a bone china cup and saucer, two lace doilies and four candy bars but had eaten the candy bars. The nice young man said that was just fine.

Next stop was at Many Glacier, where — like dozens of other awe-struck visitors — we sat in the hotel lobby and stared across a lake at a most spectacular mountain. How convenient, to have such a view where you can gaze at it in comfort! One man seemed to be defying that mountain silently to take one step toward the hotel, just one, and he'd fix it. We suspected that the view was the reason for putting the hotel there.

From there we went on a hike to Grinnell Lake, conducted by a Park naturalist. The hike was easy — most of it was by boat. One ride took us to the end of Swiftcurrent Lake and another along Josephine Lake. We were relieved to find that passengers didn't have to portage the launch. Someone had thoughtfully provided a boat for

154

each lake.

After a side trip to Browning, outside the Park, to see the Museum of the Plains Indian, we went back to the west side, to that haunt of my childhood, the former Lewis Hotel, by this time renamed the Lake McDonald Lodge. What a difference the years had made! Nobody wore formal clothes to dinner any more, you couldn't tell Easterner from Westerner, and we were all just travelers together, having a good time. Here, the next morning, we set out bravely for Sperry Glacier, taking our necessaries in knapsacks and leaving our other baggage locked in the car.

But this time we traveled like rich people, on horseback. Our party included five horses, a guide, and a man who led a packhorse. We arranged the night before to set out at 8:45 A.M. Our guide comforted us in the bleak gray morn by saying that we didn't really have to start then. It might rain, he said. We had assumed that, once plans were established, the horses would be stamping indignantly in the lobby at precisely the time agreed upon. It turned out that those horses hadn't been indignant about anything for years and wouldn't have cared if we had called off the trip entirely. There were times, in the next few hours, when we wished they had tried to talk us out of it.

It didn't really rain on the way to Sperry Chalets but we got wet anyway, because the brush along the way was dripping. Wet clouds sagged down from the mountain peaks.

My horse developed a freak stunt when we started to ford a stream. He went into reverse. Nobody had ever told me what to do in a case like that. I know how to start and stop a horse and how to shift him into high gear if he has one, but what do you do with a horse that goes backward?

155

For a while it looked as if I'd have to head him downhill in order to make him go up it.

How fine it would be, Kay and I kept telling ourselves, to get to the chalet. How nice to sit before a roaring open fire among jolly, athletic mountain climbers, bubbling with youthful zest as they dried their socks before the leaping flames and made the rafters ring with song as they raised glasses high. This thought cheered us upward and onward.

So did our guide. He approved of us because we were going up to a glacier. "People have got too soft," he fretted. "Used to be they hiked or rode all over — there're a thousand miles of trails in the Park. Now it's all cars, cars, cars, and they won't make no effort to go nowhere, they expect us to bring the glaciers down to them."

When, at last, we saw the chalets perched high above us on a cliff, we knew how stout Cortez felt, silent upon a peak in Darien, and how the Pilgrim Fathers welcomed their first glimpse of Massachusetts. We felt that our triumphant arrival should be greeted with a great burst of music — something by Wagner, accompanied by the full Metropolitan Opera orchestra and the costumed chorus in full cry, waving spears.

Instead we got immediate cups of hot coffee, which was more to the point.

There were no healthy, jolly mountain climbers drying their socks by an open fire. Sperry Chalets had oil heaters — the oil was toted up on packhorses — because it wouldn't do to hack down the forest primeval for firewood. It's part of the scenery. The only potential mountain climbers were the not terribly jolly Glacier Girls, Kay and Dorothy, and we weren't feeling very healthy. My right hip was slightly dislocated, and Kay said her solar

156

plexus squeaked.

Still, riding was better than walking.

All my life I have worried about being late. So I had carefully planned that we would get to Sperry the day the chalets opened, before they became crowded. We did arrive on opening day — July 1 — and this was an awful mistake. It was still winter up there, with lots of snow and vast sheets of ice. Some days ahead of us, four women and a boy who were going to run the place had arrived. They were all dying to make us happy. Every time they saw us, the ladies gave us a snack, and there were substantial meals as well. The boy spent his waking hours trying to make the oil heater work in our sleeping quarters. We had expected to stay two or three days, but a look at the snow and ice and rain-clouds persuaded us otherwise.

"Let's get up to that glacier and get it over with," said Kay grimly. "It's three miles, the guide book says."

We never made it. So early in the season, nobody had cleared the trail. Wading through snow with ice water running under it is different from riding a horse that does the wading. There was a broad, steep slope ahead, a talus slope where broken rocks had slid down the mountain in a great swoop. The trail across that swoop was visible in places, but the walking was worse than on the level because of snow patches with slippery bear grass underneath. We crossed two of the patches at considerable risk to life and limb and then sat down to consider the immediate future. We really needed a bulldozer, some ropes, a regiment of trained mountain troops, and more stamina. We had nothing to lose by changing our minds. Mine was changed before we crossed the first snow patch. The second one converted Kay. Feeling that we had some rights as that season's pioneers, we named the snow

157

patches Burnham's Folly and Johnson's Doom.

"A girl could get her pretty neck broke here," Kay remarked, looking down into the abyss. We teetered perilously back to the chalet for hot coffee and dry socks. Then from the porch we looked down through gray clouds toward Lake McDonald, six moist miles away, and sighed.

With my elbows on the railing I recited, "The blesséd damozel leaned out from the gold bar of heaven; she had three lilies in her hand, and the stars in her hair were seven."

This didn't cheer us up. I was wearing wet wool slacks and two wool shirts over winter underwear, and with that rig lilies would have been inappropriate.

Kay remarked wistfully, "Now I know how a kitten feels at the top of a telephone pole. How soon can we get out of here?"

"We can phone down and have the man with the horses up here by noon tomorrow or earlier," I suggested.

"I'd rather walk and get it over with," Kay decided, but she agreed that we'd better wait until morning.

It didn't rain *all* the time we were at Sperry. For a while it hailed instead. After a bountiful supper we were sitting by the oil stove in the sleeping chalet, moodily greasing our shoes, when a clatter on the porch made us jump. Three mountain goats were staring in at us. They ran, with Kay after them; she peered cautiously around the corner of the building to find them peering cautiously back at her. For the rest of the evening they played ring-around-the-chalet, clattering the length of the porch and peeking in the window.

Since those goats are up there anyway, with time on their hands (or hooves), why couldn't they have broken a trail for us to the glacier? But no, they waste their time

158

playing childish games and staring through windows at startled ladies who are trying to get into their winter pajamas by the oil heater and wondering whether five Hudson's Bay blankets will be enough. (With six, you can't turn over).

Next morning, for a change, the sun was shining. Not much, but some, just to prove it could. The management offered enough breakfast for twelve people, but we prudently ate enough for only four or five.

The trip down, on foot, took four hours. Now and then we peeled off a layer of wool as we advanced into the temperate zone. I told Kay how elegantly people had dressed for dinner at that hotel back in the years when I coudn't afford to eat there but peeked in the window like a mountain goat.

When we arrived, we were going to look like a couple of tramps. Somehow we managed to work up quite a rage about a purely imaginary conversation that would take place if the management didn't like our looks at lunchtime. Our car was there, our baggage was there, we had been there two nights before; we were not going to get all slicked up for lunch, because we were hungry. No such conversation took place. Nobody cared how we looked. Aw, shucks. How times had changed in Glacier National Park!

We were relieved not to meet our guide again, because our failure to reach Sperry Glacier had put us into the category of tourists he didn't like, those who expect the glaciers to come down to the road to be looked at. And why shouldn't they? Glaciers do move, although not very fast. They're big; they can just shove things out of their way. And furthermore, they know the country. We did our best. Let *them* co-operate a little.

Although I've spent most of my life within a reasonable

159

distance of Glacier National Park, I've never yet reached one of its glaciers. The only glacier I have ever set foot on was in the Southern Alps of New Zealand, where they make it easy. You stay at an elegant hotel with the whole front made of glass so you can stare and stare at the glory of Mount Cooke, called "Cloud Piercer" by the native Maoris. You go to the Tasman Glacier, eighteen miles long, in a five-passenger plane that has skis for landing on snow. And there you are. Now *that's* the way to visit a glacier.

What to Do With Snow

EVEN WHEN WE DIDN'T HAVE MUCH ELSE, we had early winters, late springs, and snow. Snow makes pretty good insulation when it packs around a low-slung house. Snow permitted us to make ice cream without ice late in the spring. Snow made it possible for lumberjacks with laboring horses to pull logs out of the deep woods.

Aside from these uses, snow was an awful nuisance, to which the people of Whitefish adjusted.

We waded through snow hip deep to a tall Swede. Wagons traded their wheels for big runners. Railroad locomotives used huge mechanical devices to remove snow from the tracks. Everybody shoveled. Nobody had to clear driveways when nobody had a car.

For children, snow was even fun. Whitefish had little hills, big hills and sleds. Kids with Flexible Flyers put on airs. I was rather meek with a Firefly, but all sleds with a steering bar worked the same way. There was no danger from traffic — we could see a plodding team pulling a wagon in plenty of time — but we had to avoid stumps. If you have ever hit a solid object with your skull while belly-whopping, you will understand.

Skis first came to my attention when I was home for Christmas during my sophomore year in college. A couple of boys I knew had them. Nobody quite knew what to do with them. We had never seen skiing in the movies or in real life, so we tried to ski as we had learned to swim — simply by doing it. Experts did not do it that way. They had a lot of fancy doo-dads that we didn't know about and local hardware stores didn't try to sell.

We wouldn't have known what to do with ski poles. We wore our ordinary snow-shoveling shoes, overalls and heavy jackets. The skis had no devices to hold our feet; each had a plain strap through which we slipped the toe of the shoe, and that was it.

Of course the big problem was not skiing technique but simply trying to keep one's feet on the skis, very tricky with snow balled into ice under the heels. A peculiar muscular convulsion is required to get the skis moving forward under these conditions, without poles. So we did our skiing on the slope into the hollow (or gully, ravine or draw) by my house. The hollow was bridged by a trestle, held up by wooden supports, which good sense dictated that we should avoid if we got that far.

Once I did get that far, in spite of small obstacles like bushes sticking up through the snow. Without knowing how to turn, I did turn by leaning to one side, thus avoiding

161

the trestle supports. Dizzy with success, I fell down. Then I gave up skiing.

But a new dawn was coming. I finished college and moved out of the state. While my back was turned, the snow kept falling on Whitefish and adventuresome males went on fooling with skis. From out of town came a few who understood the technique. As the winters drifted by, they built a rough cabin called Hell Roaring Ski Camp. Sensible name; it was on Hell Roaring Mountain, named for a noisy creek.

In 1936, Lloyd Muldown went clear to Europe to get the latest scoop on this sport. He brought back information on European skiing and books about the latest methods as used in Switzerland.

People were swarming over the snowy mountain slopes north of Whitefish, marking trails, skiing, falling down. Word was spreading; so was enthusiasm for the sport. In 1939 the first Montana High School Ski Tournament was held at Hell Roaring.

A ski resort began to develop. Hell Roaring became Big Mountain. This is a pity. An older generation disapproved of bad words like "hell," but skiers certainly don't. The sissy new name has not hampered the expansion of the ski resort, however.

The town long ago stopped swearing at snow. Loyal inhabitants now Think Snow and some even pray for it, because good skiing conditions bring prosperous visitors. Snow depth is reported by inches of pack with so many inches of powder on top. Anxious skiers all over the country take note.

At the Big Mountain resort and downtown motels visitors can loll in luxury and eat high on the hog. A bit of shopping will disclose hot tubs, saunas, heated indoor swimming pools. (Remember an earlier generation taking a Saturday night bath in a wash tub in front of the kitchen range. That was pretty darn nice, too.)

Snow, with downhill and cross-country skiing, is only one of the attractions. Ice fisherman like winter too.

Big Mountain has day and night skiing, lodgings ranging from rustic to regal, even a day care center.

When skiing is finished, in the spring you can still ride way up in a chair lift, rest your eyes on distant lakes and valleys, catch your breath at the sight of beargrass blooming like pale torches among the trees.

Whitefish Lake is right where it always was, and just as cold, but swimmers no longer have to dress in the bushes.

The town boasts that all in one spring day, if your strength holds out, you can ski Big Mountain, then ride down to the valley floor and play 18 holes of golf. Wait a bit before taking an invigorating plunge into the lake. We used to boast about swimming before June 1, but we never claimed we enjoyed it.

In summer the lake is bright with sailboats and noisy motorboats pulling water skiers.

Whitefish has become a year-round playground for visitors from far and near. A lot of them liked it so well that they bought land and moved in.

Condominiums and luxury apartments have grown where porcupines and grouse once lurked. Early city councils dealt with getting wooden sidewalks built downtown; present councils deal with developers determined to circumvent laws governing sewage disposal.

Visitors call Whitefish a "pretty little town." A Chamber of Commerce brochure calls it "quaint." Well, I do declare! They should have seen it when it was too raw to be pretty and too new to be quaint, when it was boisterous

163

and howling and always outgrowing its britches.

My hometown and I grew up together. Now we go our separate ways. Sing a song of laughter, a pocketful of wry.